Excellence
in
First-Year Writing
2019/2020

The English Department Writing Program
and
The Gayle Morris Sweetland Center for Writing

Edited by
Dana Nichols

Published in 2020 by Michigan Publishing
University of Michigan Library

Please send permission requests to:

Michigan Publishing
1210 Buhr Building
839 Greene Street
Ann Arbor, MI 48104
lib.pod@umich.edu

ISBN 978-1-60785-582-8

Table of Contents

Excellence in First-Year Writing

Excellence in First-Year Writing

EDWP Writing Prize Chairs

Hannah Bredar

Elana Maloul

EDWP Writing Prize Committee

Annette Beauchamp

Ani Bezirdzhyan

Hannah Bredar

Maia Farrar

Marianna Hagler

Martha Henzy

Jonathan Holland

Molly Keran

Patricia Khleif

Elana Maloul

Michelle Sprouse

Sweetland Writing Prize Chair

Dana Nichols

Sweetland Writing Prize Committee

Angie Berkley

Jimmy Brancho

Gina Brandolino

Raymond McDaniel

Carol Tell

Sweetland Writing Prize Judges

Scott Beal

Cat Cassel

Louis Cicciarelli

Shuwen Li

Simone Sessolo

Naomi Silver

Administrative Support

Laura Schulyer

Aaron Valdez

Winners List

Feinberg Family Prize for Excellence in First-Year Writing

Arianne Kok, "Unfaltering Autonomy: Feminist Doubling within *Frankenstein*"
Nominated by Matthew Bellamy, ENGLISH 124

Caroline Carr, "A Pathway to Success for the Privileged: Exploring Inequity within Chicago Schools"
Nominated by Kamaria Porter, ENGLISH 125

Sofia Perri, "Tyler, The Creator and Hip-Hop's Homophobic Dilemma"
Nominated by Aleksandria Marciniak, ENGLISH 125

Matt Kelley Prize for Excellence in First-Year Writing

Grace Brown, "An Open Letter to Bill Donohue, President of the Catholic League: Concerning Your Editorial on the Equality Act"
Nominated by Genta Nishku, COMPLIT 122

Jackson Mott, "Life Sucks, And Then You Die"
Nominated by Cat Cassel, LSWA 125

Excellence in Multilingual Writing

Hao Chen, "Reasons for Digital Piracy Behavior and Strategies to Stop It"
Nominated by Allison Piippo, WRITING 120

Kyungrae Lee, "Do Not Take Anything Slightly"
Nominated by Scott Beal, WRITING 120

Excellence in the Practice of Writing

Alyssa Huang, "黄瑞欣 "Huángruìxīn""
Nominated by Gina Brandolino, WRITING 100

Dallas Witbeck, "I am a Twig in a Nature of Drawing: The Story of Finding my Major" *Nominated by Hannah Webster, WRITING 100*

Nominees

Feinberg Family Prize (Analytic Argument)

Student	Instructor
Samantha Bakes	Carlina Duan
Remi Beaufils	Jonathan Holland
Hannah Davies	Rebecca Hixon
Jenna Elwing	Lazarus Belle
Blair Fields	Cherline Bazile
Karena Holmstrom	Katherine Beydler
Lily Karson	Vincent Longo
Arianne Kok	Matt Bellamy
Ross Ladis	Robert Bruno
Sydney Peterson	Robert Bruno
Samantha Post	Jonathan Holland
Mary Clare Shay	Charlotte Rutty
Sarah Stahlberger	Emily Saidel
Bassil Syed	Charlotte Rutty
Soumya Tejam	Luiza Duarte Caetano
Charles Tuley	Surabhi Balachander
Damiya Kaul Verma	Katy Rossing

Feinberg Family Prize (Narrative Argument)

Student	Instructor
Caroline Carr	Kamaria Porter
Emma Cary	Surabhi Balachander
Chase Cohn	Aaron Burch
Anya Eydelman	Michelle Sprouse
Hope Garcia	Aaron Burch
Noah Gross	Cherline Bazile
Jalen Gu	Carlina Duan

Student	Instructor
Michael Ivey	Aaron Burch
Jinyi Lan	Adelay Elizabeth Witherite
Nathan Lee	Emily McLaughlin
Xinyuan Liu	Michelle Sprouse
Jack Mukhtar	Michelle Sprouse
Rachel Russell	Aaron Burch
Lamese Saab	Aaron Burch
Rachel Thomas	Adelay Elizabeth Witherite
Darius Vahabzadeh	Adelay Elizabeth Witherite
Zhike Wang	Charlotte Rutty
Elizabeth Yang	Constanza Contreras Ruiz
Angela Young	Aaron Burch

Feinberg Family Prize (Research-Based Argument)

Student	Instructor
Mary Rose Azar	Aaron Burch
Julia Bentley	Aaron Burch
Vincent Doan	Aaron Burch
Brooke Drost	Martha Henzy
David Elyas	Aaron Burch
Ali Eter	Michelle Sprouse
Tyler Ezell	Emily Saidel
Whitney Flickinger	Kamaria Porter
Seth Friedman	Matt Bellamy
Marian Fu	Aaron Burch
Wyatt Gilbert	Aaron Burch
Sophie Goldberg	Aaron Burch
Lindsay Grajek	Aaron Burch
Dakota Hawkins	Elizabeth McNeill
Lina Jeffery	Jonathan Holland

Student	Instructor
Morgan Kmety	Katherine Hummel
Penny Lam	Constanza Contreras Ruiz
Grace Linenger	Jonathan Holland
Seamus Mulready	Aleksandra Marciniak
Sofia Perri	Aleksandra Marciniak
Abdullah Ramzan	Aaron Burch
Georgia Richardson-Smaller	Katherine Hummel
Cole Riggle	Jonathan Holland
Sadie Rosenberg	Michelle Sprouse
Justin Schneider	Jonathan Holland
Ethan Scholl	Katherine Hummel
Andrew Sivin	Kamaria Porter
Ryan Song	Jonathan Holland
Arundhathy Suresh	Luiza Duarte Caetano
John (Jack) Tumpowsky	Jonathan Holland
Tim Wang	Robert Bruno
Aaron Wiesel	Jonathan Holland
Catherine Zhang	Michelle Sprouse

Matt Kelley Prize for Excellence in First-Year Writing

Student	Instructor
Iris Arboreal	Karein Goertz
Allison Bell	Esther Ladkau
Amelia Berry	Alex Tarbet
Charlotte Brown	Scott Beal
Grace Brown	Genta Nishku
Helen Bryant	Cristian Capotescu
Zachary Burns	Elisabeth Fertig
Beth Devlin	Anthony Revelle
Clara Dobos	Alison Rittershaus

Student	Instructor
Emilia Ferrante	Mark Burde
Ryan Fisher	Srdjan Cvjeticanin
Cora Galpern	Elisabeth Fertig
Sarah Gerard	Genta Nishku
Augusta Guo	Alison Rittershaus
Mrinalini Gupta	Anthony Revelle
Quinna Halim	Lisa Levin
Jordan Halpern	Mark Burde
Cynthia Huang	Cat Cassel
Jared Hurwitz	Amelia Eichengreen
Liam Jankelovics	Vedran Catovic
Haley Johnson	Daniel Guttenberg
Sarah Kim	Esther Ladkau
Meredith Kratochwill	Ali Shapiro
Zora Kwasnik	Susan Rosegrant
Lisa Levin	Lisa Levin
Gina Liu	Jane Lynch
Bennet Lowe	James Prosser
Isaac Mangold	Ali Shapiro
Alena Manzor	Scott Beal
Will McClelland	Alex Tarbet
Jackson Mott	Cat Cassel
Daniel Schneide	Jane Lynch
Samantha Silverman	Julia Maxwell
Grant Sobczak	Vedran Catovic
Mya Strayer	Susan Rosegrant
Holly Teeters	Christopher Matthews
Phillips Zachary	Cristian Capotescu

Excellence in the Practice of Writing

Student	Instructor
Jiaxi (Chelsea) Cheng	Leslie Stainton
Elizabeth Engel	Jennifer Goltz-Taylor
Autumn Farnum	Simone Sessolo
Lailah Fritz	Jennifer Goltz-Taylor
Jennifer Hernandez	April Conway
Alyssa Huang	Gina Brandolino
Angel Li	Stephanie Moody
Wei-Tung (Tung Tung) Lin	Leslie Stainton
Kelly Lomonte	Jimmy Brancho
Abigail Nighswonger	Jimmy Brancho
Tegan Oppelt	Hannah Webster
Juan Sancho-Martinez	Gina Brandolino
Surina Sheth	Simone Sessolo
Rita Vega	Stephanie Moody
Dallas Witbeck	Hannah Webster
Yichuan (Johnny) Zhang	April Conway

Excellence in Multilingual Writing nominees

Student	Instructor
Hao Chen	Allison Piippo
Zongyu (Alex) Chen	Allison Piippo
Jingyi Gao	Shuwen Li
Kota Kondo	Shuwen Li
Kyungrae Lee	Scott Beal
Xinyi Xie	Scott Beal
Ruxin Zheng	Shuwen Li
GuangYu Zhou	Scott Beal

Introduction

Ten years ago, the Sweetland Center for Writing invited instructors of first-year writing courses in LSA to nominate their students for writing prizes, and the award-winning essays were published in a volume just like this one. This volume continues our recognition of and appreciation for excellent student writing. In their first-year writing courses, undergraduates are challenged to write complex, evidence-based essays; to give constructive feedback on their peers' essay drafts; to consider their peers' remarks as they revise their own essays; to write in several genres; and to develop rhetorical strategies suitable for addressing various audiences. They write short and long, formal and informal pieces. They develop their ability to read and respond to difficult texts. They learn to collaborate and advance their critical thinking skills. Their writing changes substantially as they make the transition from high school to college. Instructors have the privilege of witnessing to their social and intellectual growth. Few courses are as rewarding to teach! The writing in this volume exemplifies the excellence we expect from our smart and accomplished students.

All of the volumes in this series are available to instructors and students of first-year writing courses. Hundreds of students over the past nine years have used these volumes to understand what excellent writing looks like at their level, and to discover aspirational models for their own writing. In this year as in the past, all of the students nominated are to be congratulated: each achieved at the highest level. It is always difficult for the Sweetland judges to select those few essays that will get prizes and be printed here. I regret that we cannot give prizes for all of the outstanding work submitted.

Thanks are due to the many people involved in bringing this collection together. Let me begin by applauding the writing instructors who show students how to do their best work, and encourage them to push beyond what they think possible, to revise again and again until the ideas are clear and persuasive.

The students nominated for prizes undertake further revisions to make their submissions as compelling as possible. They deserve thanks for contributing to make this volume a witness to the best LSA students can produce. Gratitude is also owed to Dana Nichols, a member of the Sweetland faculty who has for many years served as volume editor. In this role she works with the Writing Prize Committee; recruits judges; coordinates the publication schedule and design with Aaron Valdez, Sweetland's Communications Coordinator; and proofreads the entire volume. Thanks to Angie Berkeley, Jimmy Brancho, Gina Brandolino, Raymond McDaniel, and Carol Tell who served as this year's Writing Prize Committee; and to Scott Beal, Cat Cassel, Louis Cicciarelli, Shuwen Li, Simone Sessolo, and Naomi Silver for volunteering to serve as judges. I am deeply grateful to all of these individuals for making this collection possible. It is a great pleasure to read the essays U-M students produce in their first years on campus, and we celebrate their achievements and contributions to making U-M a top-notch place to teach and study.

Theresa Tinkle
Director, Sweetland Center for Writing

The Rewards of First-Year Writing:

Introduction from the Chairs of the Feinberg Family Prize for Excellence in First-Year Writing

One of the opportunities afforded by English 124 and 125 is a chance for students to begin to find their voices through writing. This has much to do with formal elements of paper writing -- clarity of evidence, tone and audience awareness, the essay's structural logic, and more -- and it also fundamentally concerns the content about which students choose to write. Students are encouraged to use a variety of analytical skills to investigate issues that matter to them. This is what produces excellent writing: a personal investment that goes beyond the scope of the assignment, a curiosity that compels the writer to dig deeper, to ask more questions, to be comfortable with the *discomfort* of not finding easy answers. Before our reading began, the judges for each category gathered to discuss the qualities we were looking for in each essay. We were unanimous in our decision to center "intellectual risk" as one of our metrics for evaluating the essays submitted to this year's awards. The group of extraordinary papers nominated for this year's Feinberg Prizes demonstrated skillful execution of their assignments through the integration of research and narrative into their analyses, lucid prose, and powerful authorial voice. The winners of each category demonstrated an additional degree of depth and finesse: these essays registered the intellectual risk and creative critical thinking that is the result of when an author makes an assignment their own.

While only three papers were chosen for this award, we would like to honor all the essays nominated in the analytic, narrative, and research-based argument categories for inspiring their readers. We would also like to acknowledge the graduate student instructors who crafted the settings and assignments that laid the groundwork for this writing and for their enthusiasm for first year writing.

The three papers presented here demonstrate what first year college writing can accomplish in just the space of a single course. The Analytic Essay prioritizes writing supported by the author's own close readings of selected media. Arianne Kok's reading of *Frankenstein's* women offered a refreshing take on the popular novel, surprising the judges with its unique unpacking of both small moments in the novel and the text as a whole. The Narrative Essay asks students to draw from their own experience to begin to analyze a broader social or cultural phenomenon. The featured narrative essay by Caroline Carr marks the beginning stages of the lifelong project: the interrogation of one's own privileged access to education. This essay demonstrates a willingness *not* to find easy closure -- it suggests that acknowledging one's own position of racial and socioeconomic advantage is not a solution to a complex and deeply ingrained societal issue, but that it is a fundamental first step to discussing and ultimately changing the composition of this current educational landscape. Carr's essay offers a model for how one can embrace personal experience to support sophisticated argumentation, and simultaneously recognize its evidentiary limitations. The Research-Based Essay asks students to draw their thesis out of their engagement with a variety of sources. Sofia Perri's essay addresses the cultural complexities of hip hop and queer stigma in our current era of multimedia icons. She sits comfortably with the ambiguity and incommensurable nature of contemporary culture, supported by a rich and diverse body of research.

We hope these essays will teach instructors, students, and any others who study the craft of writing about the spaces writing can open up and encourage their readers to challenge their assumptions about what critical thinking can do.

Hannah Bredar & *Elana Maloul*
Graduate Student Mentors, English Department Writing Program

Feinberg Family Prize for Excellence in First-Year Writing

Unfaltering Autonomy:
Feminist Doubling within Frankenstein
by Arianne Kok
From ENGLISH 124
Nominated by Matt Bellamy

Ari wrote this essay in response to an assignment that asked students to think critically and originally about how authors approach the question of what it means to be good. The text Ari chose to re-examine in this context, Mary Shelley's *Frankenstein*, seems at first to be less a reflection on empathy, understanding, and doing the right thing than a cautionary tale about ambition, ignoring one's family, refusing to take the perspective of the Other, and heroically fainting when something bad happens. But early in the draft process, Ari came to me with the insight that, while the male characters of the novel were in many ways hopeless cases, the female figures exuded the agency, kindness, compassion, and decisiveness that mopey Victor Frankenstein and the bitter and Byronic Creature lack.

Ari then set about developing this observation into an analytical argument, one that posits that Shelley doubles the female figures in the book—Elizabeth, Mrs. Frankenstein, Justine, Safie, even the un-made body of the Creature's would-be bride—with their male counterparts in order to comment on the power of nurture, not nature, in shaping moral fiber. It's a refreshing take, a modern look at a classic novel that allows Ari to both close-read the text for convincing evidence and reflect grandly on gendered conceptions of what makes good parenting and why virtue gets overlooked when it is women who exude it. Ari's essay is an excellent example of an analytical argument, focused on the act of convincing throughout by strategically addressing counter-arguments and skillfully employing textual evidence to ground her own argumentative claims. It's also a prime example of how students can and do use writing to approach moral and ethical questions, some of which, like the ones Ari addresses here, are just as relevant today as they were in the Romantic age.

-- Matt Bellamy

Unfaltering Autonomy:
Feminist Doubling within *Frankenstein*

An ambitious college student. A science experiment turned sour. A terrifying chase for revenge. The world-famous story of *Frankenstein*, written in the early nineteenth century by romantic novelist Mary Shelley, is told in a way that no other book before it has. Twists, turns, and thrilling dramatic irony tell the story of overzealous and self-centered Victor Frankenstein, a young man whose dreams and aspirations lead him to chase a man-made superhuman through the Arctic some six years later. The novel, aside from being a constant bestseller and renowned classic, is laden with parallels of foiled male/female character pairs, compared against each other to reveal the themes within. Through these pairings, Shelley aims to argue that the influence of nurture on human behavior is stronger than inner nature, but that this manifests itself differently in males than in females. She claims that the latter is generally morally superior as a result, despite being seen as lesser by the former. Presented through Victor and Elizabeth, Felix and Safie, and the Creature and his desired female counterpart, the representation of women in *Frankenstein* varies significantly from men, especially concerning their upbringing and subsequent agency and behavior.

While many analysts of the novel deem the idea of nature versus nurture as the most remarkable theme, some may argue that it is unaffected by a difference in gender. There is some truth to this thought; the theme of nurture versus nature is exceptionally prominent throughout *Frankenstein*. Discussions of Shelley's story often debate which of the two holds more agency over deciding the true behaviors of an individual. While it is true that nature plays a definitive role, nurture holds to be the strongest determinant of mannerisms within people. The Creature, who grew up with little nurturing from his creator, is a direct contrast to the characters in the novel and even the author herself, whom all experienced fulfilled childhoods. However, there is more to this theme than catches the eye at first glance. There are stark contrasts between characters of the opposite sex, exemplified through actions that are incredibly contrary to the perception of those particular characters. The deeper connections to nurture and the outcomes of males and females become evident once the actions of certain characters are analyzed and compared.

The more surface-level difference between genders, however, is clearly highlighted in *Frankenstein*. Males in this novel do not see women as their equals, and Shelley has strategically included this to bolster her underlying argument. Elizabeth Lavenza, right from her first introduction into the novel as a rescued orphan, is seen as nothing but a prize to Victor and his family, like a beautiful and easily kept doll that will make their family happier - an object. Victor states that he "received [her] as made to a possession of [his] own" (Shelley 43). Her appearance and caretaking behavior is Victor's main focus of her, consistently describing her as "the comforter" of the household, with "her smile, her soft voice, the sweet glance of her celestial eyes" always present to "bless and animate" the family (Shelley 49, 45). He sees her beauty as her foremost quality. He emphasizes her passive, submissive behavior as the characteristic that makes her so attractive to him. Despite this perception that Victor has of her, Elizabeth is strong-willed and brave, constantly evading Victor's misogynistic views of her through intelligent, selfless actions.

This can be clearly seen in Victor and Elizabeth's very different reactions to the trial of Justine. Alphonse and Caroline Frankenstein raise Victor and Elizabeth in Geneva and give them what is described thoroughly as the perfect childhood. Their parents are "possessed by the spirit of kindness and indulgence" (Shelley 44). Mary Shelley's upbringing was aristocratic and privileged, and her parents likely inspired the siblings' parents, who tend to every need their children might have, providing them with ample free rein to learn. Victor, who describes his "eager desire to learn" the cause of his "vehement" passions, becomes a fragile, brooding protagonist after he isolates himself to create his Creature (Shelley 44). Once he realizes his Creature is responsible for the death of his younger brother, William, Victor shrinks into cowardice and internally refuses to attempt to lift the death penalty on Justine, the girl accused of the murder. He notes to himself that if someone tried to tell him the story of the Creature's creation, he would consider their words the "ravings of insanity," deeming Justine's fate inevitable and deciding that there is no use in trying to acquit her (Shelley 75). Elizabeth, on the other hand, boldly stands up in front of the court and expresses her assured belief of Justine's innocence, delivering a "simple and powerful appeal" of Justine's good soul and intentions (Shelley 81).

The difference here between Victor and Elizabeth is that one is too absorbed with himself to try to help a childhood friend and that the other risks apprehension and scorn to save her life. Though Elizabeth is unaware of Victor's creation, and that it is the real cause of William's death, she still fights for her friend, in such a way that seems to contradict how Victor has described her previously. Although raised as the cherished caretaker of the Frankenstein household, knowing she would be given to her brother in marriage one day, her autonomy is surprisingly uncompromised. She proves to those around her that she is resilient and willing, while Victor cannot muster enough courage to look at his mistakes without fainting in fear. Raised in the same household with the same ideals, attention, and love, Elizabeth and Victor are starkly different. Elizabeth grasps this freedom that Victor takes for granted with zeal, boasting agency, and bravery. While Victor would like to be known as an influential, revolutionary scientist with enough ambition to take him to the stars, he lacks the morality, strength, and goodness his female counterpart does.

Another interestingly foiled set of characters is introduced in the novel when Frankenstein's Creature retells his adventures and troubles as a newly created being, beginning with a family of three in whose secret hovel he lives. DeLacey, an old, blind man, and his two children, Felix and Agatha, live in a cottage in Germany, burdened with a fall from affluence and distinction. Felix DeLacey was raised aristocratic, "bred in the service of his country," having lived in Paris, "accompanied by a moderate fortune" and "possessed of every enjoyment" (Shelley 110). From his first introductions to the novel, he seems to be a good man, aiding a wealthy Turkish merchant condemned to death in escaping his sentence. However, the reader soon learns of Felix's real nature once the Turk asks him what he would enjoy as a reward for his assistance. He sees the "lovely" Safie, daughter of the prisoner, and "could not help owning to his mind," ensnared by the idea of receiving Safie as a "treasure which would fully reward his toil and hazard" (Shelley 111). His view of Safie as a "treasure" is akin to Victor's view of Elizabeth as a possession.

Safie, showered in her father's wealth and fortune, is brought up similarly to Felix, who, even though his circumstance now is that of poverty, enjoyed a childhood of comfort. Taken by her beauty, Felix affixes himself to the idea of keeping her, and Safie becomes similarly enamored, but her father forbids the lovers from uniting. He implores Safie to forget Felix, but she "[forms] her determination" and "[departs] for Germany," where she knows the DeLaceys reside. Safie ignores her father's commands, and, rather than stay and find herself trapped in a harem for the rest of her life, escapes to find her lover. Safie's agency and bravery become clear through her actions, despite being treated by her father as an obedient child and by Felix as a prize. Felix, like most men in the novel, sees beauty as the first and foremost quality of an individual. Safie's beauty immediately drew his liking to her. Anything that is not beautiful disgusts him, as the reader learns when he, Safie, and Agatha enter the cottage to the Creature speaking to their blind father. He "[darts] forward" in a "transport of fury," striking the Creature "violently with a stick" (Shelley 121). Although they are raised similarly, the pair act differently in the face of adversity. Safie is not taken by the illustrious promises of a wealthy life in Constantinople, escaping against her father's wishes and showing her strength and resilience. Felix is bewitched by the beauty in things, unable to look past them, and makes decisions based primarily on that. He has cold hatred for things that are different, while Safie eagerly chases them, plunging herself into a life that is hardly easy and hardly the same.

Victor Frankenstein has a deep revulsion for his Creature, harsher and more personal than that of Felix. Victor did not raise his creation at all, and his early years are nothing short of opposite to what the other characters experienced.

Victor faints at the sight of his creation and abandons the lab, leaving the Creature to his defenses. The Creature wanders the German countryside, alone and unknowing, trying to learn how to exist in the world without a shred of guidance or emotional connection. When he is finished telling Victor the beginnings of his life, filled with stories of murder and vengeful hatred towards humans, the Creature demands a female counterpart. He states that the creation of a female Creature similar to himself would "content" him and that his request is "peaceful and human" in nature (Shelley 129). He promises Victor that he and his counterpart will spend the rest of their lives far away from humans, never seen again. He has spent his entire life alone, banished by strangers who abhor the sight of him and neglected by the man who brought him to life, filling him with hatred and revenge towards humankind and leaving him with desires for a female partner. This concept of a male figure demanding a female counterpart is similar to the yearning of both Victor and Felix, who considered Elizbaeth and Safie, respectively, treasures and prizes. At first, Victor agrees to conceive the female counterpart, for the sake of finally getting rid of the Creature. However, as he is making her, staring at a pile of body parts with the Creature observing closely nearby, he experiences a change of heart. Victor begins to wonder what would happen if she were to become a "thinking and reasoning animal," refusing to "comply with a compact made before her creation" (Shelley 144). He considers the idea that a woman with agency will not listen to every command given to her by a man, and this terrifies him. The fact that she might not please his first Creature or heaven forbid, propagate a "race of devils" who terrify men for all generations to come drives him to "[tear] to pieces" the female Creature he has begun to create (Shelley 144, 145).

His predetermined notion that the female Creature may have thoughts, feelings, and agency is greater even than the fear of creating a second Creature. By destroying the counterpart, Victor has complete control over her autonomy, actions, and even procreation. Although one party in this crucial third parallel in the novel is never actually materialized, she personifies perhaps the most significant difference between men and women in relation to upbringing. The reader can assume, because of the future described by the Creature, that the female Creature would also receive no nurturing attention from her creator, much as the male Creature did not. The male Creature can experience full autonomy, with the ability to make his own decisions just like the other males in the story. The female Creature, however, is not even given a chance to, because the concept of an agentive woman terrifies Victor, as he would not be able to control her as he would like. The two Creatures would have been raised similarly in thought, but Victor denies the female Creature even a chance of escaping patriarchal jurisdiction.

The female Creature is a clear channel through which Victor's fear of female autonomy becomes apparent. Shelley cleverly uses this and other examples to her advantage, to show that although men in the novel see women as prizes and objects, the agency of women shines through without fail. Similar nurturing of males and females produces different results. Elizabeth and Safie, painted by the men in their lives who have similar upbringings as beacons of light and passivity, take ownership and are individualistic, bright characters. Although discreet, the inner workings of Frankenstein presented throughout the novel are devoutly feminist. Mary Shelley's upbringing is in part to thank for the air of womanly positivity imparted on the story, what with her mother, Mary Wollstonecraft, being one of the most prominent women's rights activists of the Enlightenment period. Mary Shelley wrote a story that never tires as it ages, and one that has managed to succeed continually through the years. The impact that Frankenstein has had on society is irreversible. What is to some merely a ghost story to tell at night or a fable to warn of excess ambition is to others a story of pushing through gender norms and having agency of one's actions in society. No man's view of a woman impacts her autonomy and self-sufficiency, and Mary Shelley has made that very clear.

Works Cited

Shelley, Mary. Frankenstein (*Case Studies in Contemporary Criticism*), Smith, Johanna M., Third Edition, Bedford/St. Martin's, 20 November 2015.

Feinberg Family Prize for Excellence in First-Year Writing

A Pathway to Success for the Privileged: Exploring Inequity within Chicago Schools
by Caroline Carr
From ENGLISH 125
Nominated by Kamaria Porter

When Cici came to office hours to discuss her narrative argument, I think she was on her third topic idea. This essay required students ground an argument about the U.S. education system using personal experience. Social class and educational inequality were major themes in this section of English 125, "Becoming in College." Fresh off of examining the College Admissions Scandal, Cici wanted to deepen her analysis of pathways to elite colleges beyond the infamous to the insidiously mundane. Cici's story, enlivened by her elegant use of narrative elements, brings the reader into the landscape of elite high school admissions in Chicago. As her reflection unfolds, her analysis of institutional racism and classism builds. The contrast Cici draws between her "path of gold stars and open doors" and the devastating school closings in communities of color demonstrates an advanced social analysis and critical consciousness. From my vantage point as an education scholar, this essay models how to understand your experiences within larger systems of privilege and come to an authentic and personal position that calls out for change.

-- Kamaria Porter

A Pathway to Success for the Privileged: Exploring Inequity within Chicago Schools

I shifted nervously in my seat, creating a loud squeak that reverberated across the packed auditorium. My mom gestured at me to stop, my anxious movement having generated a series of dirty looks from the rows in front of us. I returned a look of desperation to her, as if the rocking in my seat is the only thing keeping me breathing. However, catching the death glare of one particularly irritated mother in front of me, I ultimately sink back into my velvet cushion, defeated. It is the last week before I have to make my decision for which high school I will attend and I am completely unsure of what choice to make. My mother, who had reluctantly accompanied me to the other two admitted students nights, was becoming impatient, after all, there were only so many brochures a woman could hold. The two other choices were Latin, a private school known for its great academics and even greater wealth, and St. Ignatius, a private Catholic school that I had applied to in order to appease my very Catholic grandparents but had no intention of attending. Today, we were at the last information session for a school called Walter Payton, a selective public high school that was ranked best in Illinois and near best in the country. It was my top choice and I had worked my ass off to get into it, perfect grades, perfect test scores, perfect extracurriculars and yet, I had an overwhelming sense of guilt that I was taking someone else's spot. Payton was one of many schools characterized as selective enrollment, meaning that it was public and free to anyone in the city of Chicago, if they achieved high enough test scores and perfect grades. This was a very big if. The truth is that wealthy and white students make up the majority of these selective school's population due to their greater access to test prep and superior elementary and middle school education. The prospective class of '19 was no different. In a testament to the growing inequality within selective public schools, I viewed an auditorium of nearly all white students, many of whom I recognized from other private schools. For a school advertised as being a representation of Chicago's diversity, Payton had seriously faltered from its brochure. Sitting there, eagerly awaiting the upcoming information session, I not only came to the realization of the true measure of privilege I was awarded through Chicago's educational system, but the lack of privilege and support given to those only a zip code away from me.

I grew up on the northside of Chicago in a neighborhood called Roscoe Village, a place primarily defined by its proximity to Wrigley Field, the home of the Chicago Cubs. I didn't attend my local public school despite it's good reputation, instead my parents opted instead for the unconventional private Montessori school education for my sister and I. My childhood educational experience was characterized by gold stars and open doors. My teachers never failed in their ability to make sure each and every student knew that they had the potential for success as well as the support system to achieve it. I navigated elementary school blissfully unaware of the inequities that my fellow Chicago students were experiencing. Shielded by the homogeneous student body and cushioned by a pillow of privilege, it was only until middle school where the seemingly daily news of Chicago school closings and strikes chopped away at my ignorance, illuminating a crisis of funding and attention to Chicago's children.

While I was navigating the perils of middle school, a record number of Chicago Public Schools were being closed across the city. The proposed number of closings was a record 330 schools, however Mayor Rahm Emmanuel ultimately approved the closing of only 49 (Ewing). His explanation for these closings being the lack of resources available to continue funding schools whose academic performance was lacking and enrollment was dropping. The irony of course, as noted by a former CPS teacher Eve Ewing, was that the person "charged with doling out resources was condemning institutions for not having enough resources." Similarly, the statistics surrounding who these closings were affecting were beyond alarming. The population of the schools were 88% black with 71% mostly black teachers losing their job (Ewing). To give context for the latter statistic, 84% of public school teachers in the country are white; therefore, the closings significantly disproportionately affected people of color, telling black teachers that the thousands of hours of effort put into the success of their students were inadequate, and telling black students that their education was less of a priority. These closings demonstrated what I was coming to realize was the central flaw of Chicago's educational system: student outcome and perceived success is determined before a student even enrolls in school. Future performance relies simply on zip code and financial security. In contrast to my path of gold stars and open doors is a path of disadvantage that sees kids characterized as failures simply due to the socioeconomic circumstances they were born into. Instead of being assisted when they falter or fail, one incident in class, leads to the child characterized as problematic or disruptive for the rest of their educational careers. Researcher Julia Burdock-Will alludes to the fact that labeling a child "delinquent generates a process of cumulative disadvantage" in her research on disparities in academic performance in Chicago, demonstrating the true domino effect of this harmful rhetoric towards poorer students. In poorer communities this label occurs more frequently than not, with students internalizing the lack of care awarded to them and in turn lashing out due to the depressing nature of their circumstances.

Many Chicago politicians hail selective enrollment as the exception to this rule and the epitome of equity and inclusion. However, as aforementioned, there are a very limited number of spots, many of which automatically go to the highest scoring students who tend to be from wealthier and whiter neighborhoods. Additionally, the school I considered attending, Payton, has seen a decrease in enrollment of black students with 25% of its student body being black a decade ago, to only 11% today (Spielman). Beyond the statistics, it is imperative to look at the individual impact that policies such as this one generate. Admission of one less poor Black or Latino student means that that student will likely enroll in their local public school, receive a significantly worse education and in turn enroll in a worse college or not enroll in college at all. These seemingly simple changes in Chicago educational policies create an irreversible cascade of disadvantages that Chicagoans, particularly Chicago teachers, are fed up with it.

Chicago teachers continue to strike against the problems and inequities within our city's educational system. The most recent strike in October lasted eleven days and was the longest in Chicago history. The strikes resulted in increased funding to "reduce class sizes" and paid for "hundreds more social workers, nurses and librarians" as well as approving a "sixteen percent salary increase over the coming five years" (Smith). Despite the specific nature of their demands, the strike also drew attention to issues of social justice, "casting their fight as a battle for equity among the city's poor and rich families" (Smith). They see how in Chicago, one of the most segregated cities in the nation, both racially and financially, the disparity in access to good education between low and high income communities feeds a cycle of generational wealth for those on the northside of Chicago, while simultaneously generating a paralleling cycle of failure for those on the southside. The only way to alleviate this ever-growing issue is to acknowledge this privilege and reinvest in the communities we have so vehemently demonized.

Works Cited:

Burdick-Will, Julia. "Neighborhood Violent Crime and Academic Growth in Chicago: Lasting Effects of Early Exposure." *Social Forces; a Scientific Medium of Social Study and Interpretation*, U.S. National Library of Medicine, 1 Sept. 2016, www.ncbi.nlm.nih.gov/pmc/articles/PMC5678996/.

Ewing, Eve. "What Led Chicago to Shutter Dozens of Majority-Black Schools? Racism." *The Guardian*, Guardian News and Media, 6 Dec. 2018, www.theguardian.com/us-news/2018/dec/06/chicago-public-schools-closures-racism-ghosts-in-the-schoolyard-extract.

Smith, Mitch, and Monica Davey. "Chicago Teachers' Strike, Longest in Decades, Ends." *The New York Times*, The New York Times, 31 Oct. 2019, www.nytimes.com/2019/10/31/us/chicago-cps-teachers-strike.html

Spielman, Fran. "CPS CEO Jackson Concerned about Declining Black Enrollment and Rising Racial Tension at Walter Payton College Prep." *Times*, Chicago Sun-Times, 11 Oct. 2019, 405/cps-ceo-jackson-declining-enrollment-racial-tension-walter-payton-college-prep

Feinberg Family Prize for Excellence in First-Year Writing

Tyler, The Creator and Hip-Hop's Homophobic Dilemma
by Sofia Perri
From ENGLISH 125
Nominated by Aleksandra Marciniak

Sofia Perri's research-based essay began as an analytic argument assignment, for which students were asked to engage with modern notions of branding conceptualized by executives like Douglas Atkin. The goal was for students to broaden their understanding of "text" – allowing for companies, ad campaigns, CEOs, and personal brands to serve as the objects of their close reading – as well as to practice writing about topics of interest in a nuanced way.

Sofia chose to write about the American hip-hop artist, Tyler, The Creator. She approaches his "brand" by following his maturation as an artist and complexity as a human being, delineating between Tyler, The Creator and Tyler Okonma. Central to the essay is the title's dilemma; Tyler, The Creator's early work uses homophobic slurs, causing audiences' confusion when Tyler Okonma later reveals that he does not identify as heterosexual. Sofia approaches this dilemma by carefully navigating artistic intent and societal perception, and posing thoughtful questions about social norms and their violations in the creative sphere. Her work leaves its reader contemplating the interconnectedness of brand and consumer, artist and audience, and identity and persona in contemporary popular culture.

-- Aleksandra Marciniak

Tyler, The Creator and Hip-Hop's Homophobic Dilemma

"I TRIED TO COME OUT THE DAMN
CLOSET LIKE FOUR DAYS AGO AND
NO ONE CARED HAHAHHAHAHA"

-@tylerthecreator April 12, 2015 via Twitter.com

In the song "Goblin," released in 2011, Tyler, The Creator raps "I'm not weird, you're just a f****t, shame on him." (Tyler, The Creator). On his album of the same name, he uses f****t and other gay slurs a total of 213 times (Martin). This is the dilemma; Tyler, The Creator, born Tyler Okonma, does not see these words as slurs. For years, Okonma was painted as a villain to the LGBTQ community, taunting activists with his vulgar lyrics and erratic Tweets. Between being banned from the U.K. to getting called out by journalist in the music industry for his use of homophobic slurs, he has been trying to say something that contradicts this narrative all along; Okonma himself is a part of the queer community. His main identification, however, is with the hip-hop community, where the culture of toxic masculinity and homophobia has continued to form and reform over time. The outrageous behavior that he has become known for makes this information confusing to some and completely non-surprising to others. Tyler, The Creator's brand was previously determined by his blatantly homophobic lyrics but has developed over time through his maturing music and image, as well as the progressive conversations around the hip-hop community, to make him a visible queer artist.

Okonma's past use of gay slurs is alarming and insensitive to the LGBTQ community. Okonma rose to fame as Tyler, The Creator in 2011, when his rap collective Odd Future became popular within the Los Angeles music scene (Trammell). His first solo album, *Goblin*, was a catalyst for his career and criticisms; again, this album had 213 uses of gay slurs. The angry tone of these songs is intimidating and abrasive, and even encompass intentions of violence. When asked about the album's lyrics, Okonma has said "I'm not homophobic. I just think 'f****t' hits and hurts people. It hits. And 'gay' just means you're stupid. I don't know, we don't think about it, we're just kids. We don't think about that shit. But I don't hate gay people. I don't want anyone to think I'm homophobic." (Martin). His defense of the word has always been intent. In a tumultuous time for political correctness, it is hard to distinguish between surface words and the intent behind them. As stated in the interview excerpt above, Okonma tried to establish his own meaning of the gay slurs he used through a logic-based argument. His insensitivity of how the word has been used as an attack on the LGBTQ community is what caused public scrutiny. Okonma's struggle between how he was seen vs. how he wanted to be seen determined his brand as a homophobic and hateful rapper early in his career.

As a result of his early establish brand, Okonma's attitude and homophobic behaviors led to Theresa May, the former prime minister and home secretary of the U.K., banning Okonma from the region in 2015. When trying to enter the U.K. to perform at a music festival, he was handed a letter that read "Your albums *Bastard*, in 2009, and *Goblin*, in 2011, are based on the premise of your adopting a mentally unstable alter ego who describes violent physical abuse, rape and murder in graphic terms which appears to glamourise this behaviour." The letter goes on to highlight his lyrics that may inspire acts of homophobia in his audience (Shepherd). May's public disapproval of Okonma's brand was bigger than herself. As a woman in power, May's message carried the full force of a nation behind it. Her position allowed her to influence others into "calling out" Okonma's work. This ban essentially solidified his personal brand as a troubled artist, and Okonma chose to let his fans fight the backlash through social media, especially Twitter. One of his own tweets post-ban reads "*listens to last three releases in confusion*" (@tylerthecreator). The replies were flooded with fans calling May vile names and defending Okonma's earlier albums. Another criticism that Okonma faced is that he only addressed the part of the letter that outlined lyrics about violence against women. From this point on, Okonma chose to solely appeal to his cult audience, most of whom looked past the words he used and tried to understand the intent of his lyrics. Many of his supporters during this time identified as gay or bisexual and did not find his use of slurs offensive (Martin). Although the situation and ban could be seen as emotionally driven, many saw it as a logical punishment which discredited Tyler, The Creator's work and condemned his brand.

In recent years, Okonma has revealed his own sexuality and matured his brand. In the song "Garden Shed," off his 2017 album *Flower Boy*, Okonma raps "Garden shed, garden shed, garden shed, garden shed/ For the garden/ That is where I was hidin'/ That was real love I was in." (Tyler, The Creator) and on "I Ain't Got Time," he says "Next line will have 'em like, 'Whoa' / I've been kissing white boys since 2004." (Tyler, The Creator). These lyrics, along with others on the album, allude to Okonma engaging in gay relationships. The "garden shed" has been seen as the metaphorical "closet" that is referred to when someone reveals that they are part of the LGBTQ community. In the later song, he states his sexual experiences candidly and does not use a metaphor, even predicting his audience's reactions. Even before this album was released, he rapped on the 2015 song "F*CK IT", "How can I be homophobic when my boyfriend's a f*g?/ And we been hiding in the closet like our passion is fashion/ Still trying to come out." (Tyler The Creator). This lyric is much more direct but didn't receive as much attention. Why? Okonma's brand matured and grew between the early 2010s and 2017, and so did his audience. Because of his antics and homophobic brand stemming from early albums, Okonma's eventual "coming out" was discredited and thought to be a stunt for a long period of time. On his own Twitter page, he confused fans with tweets like "I TRIED TO COME OUT THE DAMN CLOSET LIKE FOUR DAYS AGO AND NO ONE CARED HAHAHHAHAHA" (@tylerthecreator). The music community could never decipher if this was his reality or one of his antics. In 2011, he was seen as an artist who did not take the queer community and their struggles seriously. So, when he tried to come out on his own confusing terms, he was not taken seriously. With his increasing visibility of his own sexuality,

Okonma's brand has grown outside of lyrics. His clothing brand, GOLF WANG, opened a physical location, his two latest albums *Flower Boy* and *IGOR* have debuted at #2 and #1 on the Billboard 200 charts, respectively, and he was the lead artist on the soundtrack of the major motion picture remake of *Dr. Seuss' The Grinch*. In 2015, he even released a gay pride shirt through GOLF WANG. He chose to use a Neo-Nazi symbol with the words "White Pride Worldwide," and recreate it with rainbow colors and the words "Gay Pride Worldwide." During the advertising phase, Okonma posed holding hands with a white male, further pushing public opinion and conversation about the shirt's design and meaning. With the increasingly public spotlight put on Tyler, The Creator, his newest supporters may never listen to his old music, instead focusing on his last two masterfully crafted and produced albums. On the other hand, this success has proved to many of his long-time fans that he has matured and has more to offer than seemingly insensitive and ignorant lyrics. Okonma's extension of his brand as a business has made him more accessible and mainstream to a wider audience who may not punish him for his past.

One argument that scholars have made against the homophobic wave in hip-hop is that intent is instinctively hurtful to the LGBTQ community. Marc Lamont Hill, an author and activist who teaches Media Studies and Urban Education at Temple University, wrote an essay titled "Scared Straight: Hip-Hop, Outing, and the Pedagogy of Queerness." Hill stresses how some artists have conformed to the hip-hop narrative of disdain towards the LGBTQ community, while others have used their lyrics as a way to push towards acceptance. This essay introduces the conversation of empowering gay rappers, and lends the listener to beg the question "Did Tyler Okonma achieve that in his work? Was it the purpose of his use of slurs?" Hill writes "Rap lyrics operate as one of the most prominent and accessible sites for transmitting antigay beliefs and values within hip-hop culture" (Hill). Although Okonma's original fans have not always seen his lyrics as offensive, his songs ultimately transmitted a message of homophobia. By changing three words in a song, he could have avoided this violent and hateful narrative. Okonma's deliberate and conscious choice to use these slurs in his early music shows us his wish to conform to his genre's long-standing culture. Even though Okonma claims the intent of his slurs was not hurtful, the subconscious message his lyrics have sent to his audience can incite feelings of contempt or hate.

Many people listen to Okonma's old lyrics and find nothing wrong because of the historical use of slurs in rap music. In Hill's essay, he adds "For example, top-selling rappers like Nas, Jay-Z, Nelly, 50 Cent, Eminem, Ja Rule, and DMX have all used terms like 'f****t' and 'homo' to disparage gay and lesbian people, as well as emasculate real and imagined enemies" (Hill). Rap culture has been a vehicle against a "common enemy" of the LGBTQ community. These artists make it clear that they want the two classifications of "rapper" and "gay man" to stay mutually exclusive. In the 80s and 90s hip-hop scene, being outed as a gay rapper was an embarrassment and career-ending catastrophe. However, the culture has now shifted to be more accepting to those breaking the traditional mold. Okonma falls into a gray area in this argument, and he has never fully cleared the air on it. Since he wasn't "out" when he released *Goblin*, is he still considered an outsider to the community? It seems like Okonma released these tracks to defend his own masculinity, rather than using it as a part of the community. Additionally, although he has eluded to his own gay relationships and queer expressions, he has never defined his sexuality along a clear line. He could still possibly identify as straight, and the conversation around his music over the last decade could take a turn to address "queer baiting." Transitioning to his later music, Okonma avoids using gay slurs as insults while outing himself in his own mysterious way. Hill's essay was written ten years ago, in 2009, and at the time there were no openly gay and popular rappers "With the exception of New York rapper Caushun, who signed a recording deal with Def Jam subsidiary Baby Phat Records in 2004 but has yet to release an album…" (Hill). Many things, such as political correctness in music, have changed since then, whether the hip-hop community likes it or not.

Since then, other queer, black male artists in the hip-hop community have constantly pushed a narrative of acceptance. These men have skyrocketed to popularity on a foundation that is in opposition to Okonma. The first artist is Kevin Abstract. Abstract is a member of the hip-hop collective and self-proclaimed boy band BROCKHAMPTON. In a radio interview, he stated "'I have to exist in a homophobic space in order to make change and that homophobic space would be the hip-hop community... So me just existing and being myself is making change and making things easier for other young queer kids.'" (Blake). Abstract raps about his fear of his mother not accepting him, and his confusion over the lack of hip-hop artists addressing sexuality. This transparency in his music is expanding the definition of who can be accepted as a rapper and make a successful career to include black, queer men. Abstract has still been known to joke about his sexual preferences and make political statements, but he has never used gay slurs in his music like Okonma. In 2018, he even appeared on stage at the music festival Coachella with the word "F****T" written across his chest. He wanted to shock and remind the audience of the hatred that word held, almost reclaiming it, but now does not use the word at all (LeBeouf and White). Yet, he still fully supports Okonma and has even tweeted "tyler the creator greatest rapper on earth." (@kevinabstract). Another artist who is constantly tied into the conversation about Okonma's past is Frank Ocean. Ocean was a member of Okonma's collective Odd Future, and the two have collaborated on many songs. After coming out in a Tumblr post in 2012, Ocean later posted on that same account about a time his dad had called a transgender waitress a f*****t. Ocean's post resonated with the LGBTQ community and proved that he was not afraid to publicly show support for his queer brothers and sisters. Okonma was actually one of the first musicians to speak publicly about Ocean's post, congratulating him and sending his support. This act was seen to many as proof that Okonma is not homophobic, and that his lyrics' intent was not meant to harm the LGBTQ community. The post led to a lawsuit between Ocean and his dad, and blew up as a case of defamation, which Ocean eventually won (Moye). The level that this case elevated to illustrates how resilient Ocean has been in the public eye as an advocate and ally. However, after his public disapproval of gay slurs and homophobia, Ocean still has and continues to be featured by and feature Okonma in songs. Ocean has not spoken publicly about this, but it seems as though he has separated Okonma's intent from his use of gay slurs. This has caused some of Ocean's own fans to turn their back on his music, claiming that he is not a true advocate and should be pushing for Okonma to apologize for his past. While other artists in a similar position as Tyler, The Creator chose to advocate for the queer community, Okonma still remains popular and is accepted by many because of his evolving brand.

Although many artists have been able to escape their past through apologies and reparations and move on, Okonma's transformation is different. He has apologized for people feeling hurt, but never for using the homophobic slurs in his early songs. His cult audience has stuck with him through the turmoil of backlash and his ban from the U.K., and he has grown his massive fan base within the last few years. This growth has changed his personal brand and has shown that an artist can turn his own image around without compromising his true beliefs about intent. However, Okonma's audience is not the same as Hill's; there will always be a scholarly perspective that says Okonma should not be praised or admired due to his history. Through Okonma's long process of revealing his sexuality, which is still going on today, he has also been an inspiration to many in the queer community, showing that one doesn't owe it to anyone to "come out" in a traditional sense and label their sexuality. But the question remains; Is Okonma "off the hook" for his use of gay slurs because he might have been gay all along? Is this situation like black people reclaiming the n-word, as critics have suggested? (Madison). Okonma's duality is what makes him Tyler, The Creator, and we will continue to see it evolve in years to come.

Works Cited

Blake, Jimmy. "Brockhampton on Changing Hip Hop's 'Homophobic Space'." *BBC News*, BBC, 31 Aug. 2018, https://www.bbc.com/news/newsbeat-45366918.

Hill, Marc Lamont. "Scared Straight: Hip-Hop, Outing, and the Pedagogy of Queerness." Review of Education, Pedagogy, and Cultural Studies, vol. 31, no. 1, 2009, pp. 29–54., doi:10.1080/10714410802629235.

LaBeouf , Shia and Ryan White. "Kevin Abstract and Shia Labeouf in Conversation: 'If All This Was over Tomorrow, I'd Still Have Those People.'" I, 3 Sept. 2019, https://i-d.vice.com/en_us/article/vb5vdj/kevin-abstract-shia-labeouf-brockhampton-interview.

Madison, Ira. "Has Tyler, the Creator Earned His Redemption?" *GQ*, GQ, 9 Aug. 2017, https://www.gq.com/story/tyler-the-creator-flower-boy-redemption.

Martin, Daniel. "Tyler, The Creator: 'My Gay Fans Don't Find My Language Offensive'." *NME*, NME, 16 June 2011, https://www.nme.com/news/music/odd-future-82-1278567.

Moye, David. "Frank Ocean Beats His Dad's $14.5 Million Libel Lawsuit Over Gay Slur Claim." *HuffPost*, HuffPost, 19 Oct. 2017, https://www.huffpost.com/entry/frank-ocean-gay-slur-libel_n_59e8f19fe4b0df10767b9de2.

Shepherd, Julianne Escobedo. "Tyler, the Creator on Being Banned From the UK: 'I'm Being Treated like a Terrorist'." *The Guardian*, Guardian News and Media, 1 Sept. 2015, https://www.theguardian.com/music/musicblog/2015/sep/01/tyler-the-creator-comments-banned-uk-freedom-of-speech.

Tyler, The Creator. "Goblin." *Goblin* (Deluxe Edition), XL Recordings Ltd, 2011. *Spotify*, https://open.spotify.com/track/7C8PNX6VQPDtUkVpRyXV8B?si=a2qGdXFxRQu6 KEEynFYHg.

Tyler, The Creator. "Garden Shed." Flower Boy, Columbia Records, 2017. Spotify, https://open.spotify.com/track/6ACiYjq5Q7e6BlhZEHz7cd?si=TubN-lKGS4aM5PuZexIKnQ.

Tyler, The Creator. "I Ain't Got Time!" *Flower Boy*, Columbia Records, 2017. *Spotify*, https:/open.spotify.com/track/430qNtapCS3Ue1yoSql1oV?si=vu6V7T3ZRX2t5vTsFjfiBQ.

Tyler, The Creator. "FUCK IT." *Cherry Bomb*, 2015. *Sound Cloud*, https://soundcloud.com/ofwgkta-official/fuckit.

Trammell, Matthew. "Cover Story: Tyler, The Creator." *The FADER*, The FADER, 7 Oct. 2015, https://www.thefader.com/2014/11/09/cover-story-tyler-the-creator.

@kevinabstract. "tyler the creator greatest rapper on earth." *Twitter*, 27 Jul. 2018, 12:16 a.m., https://twitter.com/kevinabstract/status/1022697277935108096?s=20.

@tylerthecreator. "*listens to last three releases in confusion*" *Twitter*, 26 Aug. 2015, 2:26 p.m., https://twitter.com/tylerthecreator/status/636605593931767808?s=20.

Introduction to the Matt Kelley Prize for Excellence in First-Year Writing, Excellence in Multilingual Writing Prize, and the Excellence in the Practice of Writing Prize

The first-year writing classroom is an intellectual common space at the University of Michigan that brings students from across the university to engage in a shared project of exploring new ways of thinking and writing. This year's winners impressed the judges with the creativity and elegance of their work, which exemplifies why the first-year classroom is such an energizing place to be.

I am pleased on behalf of the Sweetland Center for Writing to congratulate our winners: Grace Brown and Jackson Mott, winners of the Matt Kelley Prize for Excellence in First-Year Writing; Hao Chen and Kyungrae Lee, winners of the Excellence in Multilingual Writing Prize; and Alyssa Huang and Dallas Witbeck, winners of the Excellence in the Practice of Writing Prize.

The writing prizes depend upon the generous support of the faculty and staff of Sweetland Center for Writing. I would like to thank this year's judges: Scott Beal, Cat Cassel, Louis Cicciarelli, Shuwen Li, Simone Sessolo, and Naomi Silver. I am especially grateful to Angie Berkley, Jimmy Brancho, Gina Brandolino, Raymond McDaniel and Carol Tell, who volunteered to serve as members of the writing prize committee. Finally, I offer my sincere thanks to Laura Schuyler and Aaron Valdez, without whom the writing prizes are impossible.

We hope you enjoy these essays as much as we did, and that they offer you a glimpse into some of the tremendous talent and potential of our first-year students.

Dana Nichols
Lecturer, Sweetland Center for Writing

Matt Kelly Prize for Excellence in First-Year Writing

An Open Letter to Bill Donohue, President of the Catholic League: Concerning Your Editorial on the Equality Act
by Grace Brown
From COMPLIT 122
Nominated by Genta Nishku

Grace Brown's open letter to Bill Donohue, the President of the Catholic League, is a exemplary example of the genre of the open letter. Grace uses engaging language and fine-tuned close reading skills to break down Donohue's writing, his argument and the rhetorical tools used, and demonstrate the flaws in his logic. In doing so, Grace drives home the point that such statements can perpetuate hate for LGBTQ+ groups, and also teaches readers how to become better critical thinkers and readers themselves. The essay combines personal experiences and observations with outside research, thus providing a richer and more diverse set of evidence to support the argument made, and also drawing in readers more.

-- Genta Nishku

An Open Letter to Bill Donohue, President of the Catholic League: Concerning Your Editorial on the Equality Act

Dear President Donohue,

As a young girl, I was always proud of my Catholic identity. In church and at home, I was told that a person's job is to honor God through charity, love, and acceptance, but as I've grown and as I continue to grow, it has become clear that faith, no matter the denomination, has the potential to be used as justification for personal biases. In the name of faith, I've seen parents denounce their gay children. In the name of God, I've seen the bruises of trans women attacked on the streets. In the name of religious freedom, I've seen friends lose their jobs, their homes. I've seen it all. Abuse. Rejection. Hatred. For a cause that is founded on the ideals of love. Of course, I do not mean to insinuate that all followers of religion act in such a way; in fact, most offer members of the LGBTQ+ community the same love that they would any other human being. I am ashamed that a man of your influence has chosen to misrepresent the members of your faith by perpetuating an attitude of bigotry and discrimination through irresponsibly broad and unfactual claims that you choose to embody in your editorial, including (but not limited to) the notion that queer identities are voluntary, the false claim that the Equality Act equates to affirmative action for gays, and the ignorant assumption that most people would agree with your reprehensible outlook on the rights of LGBTQ+ Americans.

According to your interpretation of the Equality Act, the goal of its supporters is to undermine the Religious Freedom Restoration Act (RFRA) by "allowing gay rights to trump religious rights." Reading these words, I am shocked that someone could logically conclude that civil rights for one group would in any way result from a reduction in the rights of another. In reality, the Equality Act that you are so opposed to would offer members of the LGBTQ+ community, including those that are also members of the Catholic faith, a level of dignity that we have not yet been afforded. During the course of our country's history, LGBTQ+ people have been treated as second-class citizens. Despite recent strides in the fight for equality, such as the recognition of gay marriage by the supreme court in 2015, many members of the LGBTQ+ community are vulnerable to various forms of discrimination.

> "In most states in this country, a gay couple can be married on Saturday, post their wedding photos to Instagram on Sunday, and lose their jobs or get kicked out of their apartments on Monday just because of who they are."
>
> David Cicilline, D-R.I.

The Equality Act aims to add "gender identity" and "sexual orientation" to the classes protected from discrimination in the Civil Rights Act of 1964. It also provides additional protections to all marginalized groups of people by specifying that discrimination is illegal in "retail stores, emergency shelters, banks, transit and pharmacies, among other places" (Fitzsimons). The only mention of the RFRA is the clarification that religious liberties are prohibited from being used as a license to discriminate (Fitzsimons). If you believe that it is a violation of your religious freedom for the government to declare using your personal beliefs as an excuse to deny another person their civil rights, then your definition of religious freedom is deeply flawed.

In your editorial, you mentioned that there were instances where "disparate treatment on the basis of achieved characteristics such as sexual orientation and gender identity can be justified." By referencing the notion that gender identity and sexuality are the result of choice, Mr. Donohue, you are reducing the experience of an entire community to the assumption that we want to be as different. As a girl who grew up Catholic, I never *wanted* to be gay. In fact, it was the one thing about myself that I wanted to change for the longest time. I thought that because it was considered "sinful" for me to have a girlfriend, I would be considered a bad person for falling in love. I was filled with a constant fear of authenticity, as it would result in disapproval from those that I cared for most in the world. This experience is a common one, and it is often an added challenge when individuals such as yourself treat people in the LGBTQ+ community as a disease after learning of their identity. In stating that there are situations where it is acceptable to treat us differently, you are allowing for this pattern of hatred and aggression to continue.

I distinctly recall that you referenced an example where religiously devout parents should have the right to deny their child seek the professional counseling by "a woman who has acquired male genitalia." In what situation would this be an acceptable course of action? Why is someone's genitalia a qualifier for their ability to perform their job? Better yet, how is it anyone's right to ask about *anyone's* genitalia, no matter their gender identity? This course of action the equivalent of asking a doctor if they are circumcised or not - it should not matter, as it has no pertinence to their quality of work. You provide no justifiable situation where LGBTQ+ people should be discriminated against. In fact, there is no scenario where it would be remotely acceptable to treat LGBTQ+ citizens in a discriminatory manner because, similarly to sex, race, and ethnicity, an individual's status as LGBTQ+ is a trait that they are born with, allowing for the *logical* conclusion that an LGBTQ+ person's civil rights are of similar value. We are people, and we deserve to be treated as such. The practice of discriminatory treatment on the grounds of religion, race, sex, or ethnicity is viewed as ludicrous by a majority of our nation's population - why should unequal treatment of LGBTQ+ individuals be perceived any differently?

> "The burden should be on those who want to treat LGBT equality differently from racial (or gender) equality when it comes to religious exemptions to explain why that differential treatment is justified, and claims based on the good faith of those who object to the application of LGBT equality mandates on religious grounds simply do not cut it."
>
> Carlos A. Ball, Legal Expert and LGBTQ+ Advocate

Not only is your piece hateful and inflammatory; it is also wildly unfactual. A central point that you aim to make is that the Equality Act is essentially affirmative action for gays. Beyond its inclusion in your horrendously offensive title: "Affirmative Action for the Sexually Confused?", the notion of affirmative action comprises roughly one third of your piece. In actuality, the Equality Act makes no mention of affirmative action. Your case that the Equality Act would usher in an era of "preferential treatment" for LGBTQ+ Americans rests entirely on the assumption that adding gender identity and sexual orientation to the list of groups protected by the Civil Rights Act would in some way force institutions to implement a new affirmative action protocol of sorts. This is logistically improbable simply because it is incredibly unethical to inquire about an individual's sexual orientation or the specifics of gender orientation (such as a previous transition or intersex status) in a vocational environment. If we as a society continue to view these practices as invasive, then a significant barrier to affirmative action for the queer population of the U.S. would be ever-present. Following this logic, it is actually likelier that the Equality Act would *prevent* the LGBTQ+ affirmative action that you are so against. Your negative fixation on "affirmative action for gays" portrays a pathetic attempt to employ controversial vernacular to reach a broader audience. Because the proposed legislation has no intention of inciting affirmative action, the use of the phrase in your editorial is essentially the exaggeration of a buzzword for the sake of media traction. These are the type of tactics that do not garner a supportive audience, and if you truly aim to act in accordance with the interests of Catholic Americans, you would present your argument in a respectful and responsible manner.

In addition to the misuse of affirmative action, you claim in this piece that "if most Americans knew what [the Equality Act] is really about, they would not support it." This is simply untrue. According to a 2017 survey of American values, most Americans do, in fact, support the notion of "laws that would protect gay, lesbian, bisexual, and transgender people against discrimination in jobs, public accommodations, and housing" (Vandermaas-Peeler et al.). Not only do a majority of Americans favor legislation similar to the Equality Act, all major religions practiced in the United States (save for Jehovah's Witnesses, who are split 50-50 on the issue) contain a majority of supporters for nondiscrimination laws concerning LGBTQ+ individuals. This would include the Catholic laity, who you claim to represent. Furthermore, six in ten Americans oppose service refusals on the basis of religious beliefs, signifying once again that you represent a vocal minority on the issue of LGBTQ+ rights (Vandermaas-Peeler et al.). What has possessed you to present a viewpoint that statistically isn't Catholic in the slightest? Why have you chosen to ignore the voices of your people?

"It is easy to overlook (or forget) - as our society grapples, in particular, with contemporary controversies pitting LGBT equality against the rights of speech, association, and to the free exercise of religion of those who oppose that equality - that our nation through the decades has repeatedly dealt with difficult questions related to how best to balance the equality rights of some against the liberty interests of others."

Carlos A. Ball

The LGBTQ+ civil rights movement faces similar challenges to the movements that have preceded it; from the Civil Rights Act of 1964 to Title IX, movement towards protecting the civil rights of marginalized groups has faced opposition on the grounds of civil liberties such as freedom of speech, association, and religion (Ball 237). However, in previous cases, justice has prevailed, allowing for religious liberties to remain intact while providing underrepresented groups of Americans with the civil rights that they should have been entitled to in the first place. LGBTQ+ rights *will* be won, in a matter of time. I have faith that those who truly believe in equality for all Americans will fight for what is right. Do you want to be remembered as an individual on the wrong side of history? The Catholic League claims to fight for civil rights, so why make the exception when it comes to members of the LGBTQ+ community? There are gay Catholics. There are transgender Catholics. There are nonbinary Catholics. There are Catholics and non-Catholics who fit into every possible identity under the rainbow. It would be foolish to deny *anyone*, especially people of your own faith, the rights that you have likely taken for granted, Mr. Donohue. I hope that you can learn to emulate the Catholic values that you claim to represent and offer support to a group of people who have spent history being endlessly torn down.

Sincerely,

Grace "Cecilia" Brown

St. Mary Magdalen Parish in Kentwood, MI

References

Ball, Carlos A. "Against LGBT Exceptionalism in Religious Exemptions from Antidiscrimination Obligations," *Journal of Civil Rights and Economic Development* vol. 31, no. 2 (March 2018): p. 233-246. HeinOnline, https://heinonline.org/HOL/P?h=hein.journals/sjjlc31&i=249.

Donohue, Bill. "Affirmative Action for the Sexually Confused?" Catholic League, 12 Mar. 2019, www.catholicleague.org/affirmative-action-for-the-sexually-confused/.

Fitzsimons, Tim. "Democrats Reintroduce Equality Act to Ban LGBTQ Discrimination." NBCNews.com, NBCUniversal News Group, 13 Mar. 2019, www.nbcnews.com/feature/nbc-out/democrats-reintroduce-equality-act-ban-lgbtq-discrimination-n982771.

Jones, Robert P., Daniel Cox, Rob Griffin, Alex Vandermaas-Peeler, and Molly Fisch-Friedman. "Emerging Consensus on LGBT Issues: Findings From the 2017 American Values Atlas." PRRI. 2018.

Matt Kelly Prize for Excellence in First-Year Writing

Life Sucks, And Then You Die
by Jackson Mott
From LSWA 125, Nominated by Cat Cassel

Jackson's visual analysis examines a painting, *The Dead Soldier*, that hangs in the University of Michigan Museum of Art. He looks at how the positioning and expressivity of the three figures in the painting play with degrees of detail that are, because of the very specific medium of the painting and the way that it freezes a moment in time, meant to convey to the reader intense grief but also the banal (and yes, brutal) finality of death. This analysis is stunningly rich in its consistent attention to HOW the visual details come together to form an impression on the reader. For instance, I love the attention given over to how the different figures are positioned-- the soldier "like a rag doll" or the bonnet splayed on the ground suggestive of some preaction. The argument also goes in some weird, but intriguing, directions: Jackson focuses on the tension between the widow's face--relatively empty of intricate details that would individuate her--and the baby's face--which stares out at and directly confronts the viewer--and suggests that the facelessness of the widow allows us to occupy her emotional stance a bit more freely, while the baby's confrontational stare amplifies a sense of naivety towards death. This does exactly what a compelling visual analysis does, in that Jackson has shown the reader something that is rather implicit in the text, but which makes perfect sense now that he has walked the reader through HOW those details are suggestive of his overall thematic. He has shown his reader something that is bizarre and that needs accounting for. And even down to the sentence-level, Jackson takes care to structure his analysis and provide thick description so that one can see the painting in one's mind's eye.

-- *Cat Cassel*

Life Sucks, And Then You Die

One of the unfortunate truths of existence is that it is constantly ending. Worse still is that even though we are all guaranteed to die, it is far from guaranteed that our existence before death will be one free from suffering. The human experience is rife with miseries, and it is necessary for survival to find a way to wrestle with it all. For some creative-minded individuals, this means deconstructing the perils of living and reconfiguring them into art. Examples of emotionally charged works abound, but nowhere is the tortured spirit of humanity presented more poignantly than in Joseph Wright of Derby's 1789 work *The Dead Soldier*. With its devastating portrayal of a family shattered by war, *The Dead Soldier* illustrates the brutal nature of human existence. To achieve this sentiment, the piece is unflinching in its attention to the uncomfortably intimate details of suffering. Specifically, the facial and bodily characteristics of the subjects—the soldier, the wife, and the child—each provide a unique perspective on how we experience our humanity.

In *The Dead Soldier*, a beautiful portrait is created with earthy, subtle colors and an unbalanced composition, with the perspective focusing mainly on the three human subjects while the lush background fills the auxiliary role of providing context. The careful brushstrokes of the oil painting are reminiscent of regal portraits of European royalty, giving the piece a grandeur and emotional intensity unable to be captured by another medium. In the foreground, a woman, infant, and soldier are each shown in varying positions. The titular soldier rests facedown on the forest floor, his bright red uniform with shining white and gold accents creating a brilliant contrast with the surrounding environment and giving historical background as it reveals his identity as a fallen soldier in the American Revolutionary War. No bloodshed is shown, but the pure devastation shown in the woman makes it clear her partner is gone. The woman, assumed to be the soldier's wife, is shown crouching down next to the soldier in a dark, elegant dress, her body arched forward so her head may rest on his arm. Perhaps in an effort to show the suddenness of her reaction, her bonnet is shown on the forest floor having fallen from her head. Her body appears fragile, broken by the sorrow and despair known only by a widow. As with the soldier, her face remains hidden from view. Resting in her lap is the third and final subject of the piece: the child. The infantile boy is posed looking directly at the viewer, an expression of calm cast across his face, a direct contradiction of the intentional anonymity of his parents. He appears to have fallen away from breastfeeding, perhaps symbolizing the struggle for resources to come without his father's support, and is now seen grasping onto the fingers of the soldier as they're held up by the mother. The detailed physical interaction of these three characters provides a simple yet deeply moving image of a family faced with a tragic situation.

In contrast with the harrowing nature of the foreground, the background appears serene. Behind the family rests a large tarp, appearing light brown and rough in texture. As it hangs from the trees, the tarp acts as a symbol of refuge, concealing them from view and protecting them from further harm at the hands of an unforgiving world. Large trees stand stoically throughout the piece, their leaves a lovely mix of green, orange, and yellow in transition from summer to autumn, representative of change to come. The natural lighting of the piece gives the scene a gentle glow, showering the family with warmth and invoking feelings of contentment. The lighting is also utilized as a subtle show of drama; the sun shines down on the family, signifying their importance by acting as a sort of spotlight. To the right of the family, there is a break in the tree line and a grassy clearing shown a ways away. Above the clearing, a small amount of the sky can be seen through the trees appearing light blue and cloudy, though a billow of smoke casts a dark, angry haze over the horizon. Most notable, however, is the small burst of orange-pink light emerging from the smoke, giving warmth and serenity to an otherwise catastrophic scene. Upon first glance, it appears to be a sunrise or sunset, adding to the natural beauty of the lush forest background. However, further inspection reveals it is something far less peaceful: the burning sight of an explosion. This particular use of color is excellent, as it provides contrast with the rest of the piece similarly to that of the soldier's red uniform. The deceptively inviting image is a grim reminder that no matter how stable things may appear, life always has the potential for arbitrary destruction.

What truly gives *The Dead Soldier* its powerful emotional potency is its unique positioning of the three characters' bodies and faces. By choosing to portray each with their own distinct body language and facial expression (or lack thereof), Wright captures the ways we as humans process the perils of existence and how they differ at various stages of life. In the earlier stages of life, we are incapable of understanding, or even identifying personal hardships outside of basic needs like being fed or rocked to sleep. It would be inane to assume an infant could process death and the like. Without the experience and knowledge of more concrete concepts of human interaction and the unrelenting nature of life itself, young children have a sort of blissful ignorance to what makes life so unbearable. Thus, the infant boy in the painting does not know the implications of the situation, and this is shown in the naivety on his face as he lays in his grieving mother's arms. On the contrary, adults have been through enough of life to know its unfortunate truths. While it may not affect us all in the same way, as shown by the vastly different states of the wife and soldier, death is wholly tied to our being.

To truly understand Wright's possible implications of death and its subjective effects, we must first examine the titular dead soldier. Wright paints him solemnly; the soldier is a vital piece to his larger artistic statement and thus must be given the utmost attention in order to represent and honor him properly He is shown strewn like a rag doll across the ground, his crumpled position portraying him almost as an object, but his physical characteristics tell enough of his story to understand him as a character. The aforementioned red uniform is a large example of this, as it represents the singular concrete detail we are given about his life: he was a soldier. With his decision to render the soldier facedown in the dirt, Wright forces viewers to emote with an entirely anonymous individual. A potential interpretation of this is that, in the context of war, society views soldiers as disposable blank slates. If one is killed, they are simply replaced by another citizen. They are seen as statistics in an endless game of numbers between countries rather than people with stories, experiences, hopes, and dreams. Upon his killing, the soldier's experience as a human being, and thus, his happiness, was curtailed. Never again will he embrace his wife, nor will he hold his son's hand as he learns to walk, nor will he experience laughter or excitement or friendship or love or any of the joys of humanity ever again. Though he may be barred from such experiences, it is a small silver lining that he is now free from life's seemingly endless stream of pain. He is just another person, infinitely specific in his own life, but anonymous in the eyes of death. He may finally rest, just as we all will.

Looking deeper into the piece, Wright utilizes the wife of the soldier to represent experiencing the death of a loved one. Wright envisions her with a mournful air, radiating out to the viewer. This is largely communicated by her body language: her head hangs low in sorrow, and her hands hold onto both the child and the soldier as if she lets go she may fall to pieces. One hand holds the child upright, potentially an indication to her duty to support him alone now that her partner is gone. The other grasps the soldier's wrist, raising his icy white hand so the child may have a final chance to feel their father's touch. Her face remains hidden from view as she rests it on her partner's arm; it is left up to the viewer's imagination to conjure the suffering in her expression. As with the soldier, I believe the decision to make her faceless could be to show the ubiquity of death, though in a slightly different way. While the soldier may have appeared anonymous to show that we are all the same in the sense that we all die, the wife's anonymity could be representative of the idea that we are all affected by death. Though one's own experience may be subjective, everyone bears witness to loss. Whether it be family, friends, lovers, or colleagues, it is a truth we must fight to accept that each day can, and eventually will, be someone's last. As for the wife, that world-shattering day came when her partner was killed in battle.

Finally, we come to the last of the three subjects in *The Dead Soldier*: the child. The infant is portrayed much differently than his parents in the scene.

Wright subverts expectations and breaks the pattern of anonymity by not only making his face visible but having him look directly at the viewer. The effect is jarring, as we have gone from being spared the grim details of the parents' faces to now being forced to confront the son head-on. However, this does not mean the child's face is troubling in any sense. Truthfully, it's calm and content, as a child should be. He is illustrated as carefree, and this is what sets him apart from the other characters. As previously mentioned, he is a child, so he does not know of or understand the dire implications of the situation. When he holds the hand of his father, he does not know it is lifeless. By portraying the child this way, I believe Wright could be commenting on how children are naive and innocent in the face of death. The child faces us because he is looking to us for guidance; he still has the potential to successfully endure all of life's hardships, he just doesn't know it yet. It is almost as if he is gazing through the painting to ask, "What is wrong? Why do you appear so troubled?". We cannot answer, we can only hope he will be prepared for the trials of life and death.

Wright's *The Dead Soldier* is a contemplative look at the cross-section between humanity and death. By looking solely at one family in turmoil and drawing special attention to their physical characteristics, the piece is effective in its simple focus. Because of this, it allows viewers to analyze and relate to each character individually despite its undertaking of such a huge topic as the pervasiveness of death. Its rich detail, somber tone, and evocative displays of humanity make it a sobering display of the raw human experience. It is emotionally visceral, yet wildly stimulating on a philosophical and intellectual level. What is likely the greatest point being made by Wright in *The Dead Soldier* is this: how we attempt to make sense of life's lack of sense, especially regarding its eventual end, is a massive part of what makes our human experience so unique. Existence is nothing if not finite, and we as humans must grapple with this every day we are given the privilege to exist. Regarding this truth, the wife, the child, and *The Dead Soldier* each have something to tell us. If we listen, not only to them but to each other, we just might learn to embrace death as an essential companion of life rather than its enemy.

Excellence in Multilingual Writing

Reasons for Digital Piracy Behavior and Strategies to Stop It
by Hao Chen
From WRITING 120
Nominated by Allison Piippo

Hao did a great job of developing his ideas and this paper over the course of the semester. Throughout the many revisions he did on this paper, he developed a strong organizational structure and well-developed arguments that were strongly supported with appropriate research. He gave excellent suggestions for reducing digital piracy based on the causes that he found through the research.

-- *Allison Piippo*

Abstract

Digital piracy is serious in many countries, and it has already caused huge economic losses in the past few decades. Hence, this article is to explore the reasons why consumers commit digital piracy and inform people how to avoid this behavior. The paper first focuses on whether consumers' ethical perceptions on purchasing pirated digital goods and their intentions to do that can influence digital piracy behavior, and how these two determinants are affected by other factors. It is concluded that the consumers' ethical perspectives are influenced by gender and downloader types, and that purchasers' intentions to pirate is mainly determined by their perceptions of justice, attitude toward digital piracy, perceived consequences of it and ethical or moral perceptions on it. Therefore, it is important to combine these two determinants and other related factors together in order to give an objective prediction of digital piracy behavior. Then several possible strategies are proposed based on the reasons for digital piracy.

Reasons for Digital Piracy Behavior and Strategies to Stop It

Introduction

At the beginning of this semester, I had a chat with a friend of mine and complained that textbooks in the USA were very expensive, then he suggested that I buy electronic books from an unofficial online store where the prices were much lower. That was true, but buying this kind of book might not be a wonderful idea since this action did not respect the writers' hard work. Later I found that a lot of people had similar practices all over the world: "Thailand is one country that has been placed on the priority watch list of intellectual property violators. Ten countries including Algeria, Argentina, Chile, China, India, Indonesia, Pakistan, Russia, Thailand, and Venezuela have also been identified" (Thongmak, 2017, p.2). This new way of violating intellectual property, which occurs with the development of technology, is called digital piracy.

> Some people might think that digital piracy should not be condemned too much, actually it has many negative effects on our society. Pirating of a billion dollars worth of digital products happens every day and global market revenues have declined because of digital piracy. Fifty-one point four billion dollars are lost due to software piracy around the world. Music piracy causes 12.5 billion of dollars of loss in the U.S. economy and 70,000 lost jobs for American workers…Book publishers in the United States report forty percent losses in potential sales due to book piracy. (Thongmak, 2017, p.1-2)

Hence, buying pirated digital products can undermine many types of digital product industry, so it is necessary to avoid that behavior. In order to carry out strategies to prevent it, we first need to find out why this behavior is prevalent. Consumers' ethical perceptions of purchasing pirated digital goods and their intentions to do that are two aspects for explaining why digital piracy occurs, and there are several possible solutions to stop digital piracy based on these reasons. I will focus on the two factors (consumers' ethical perceptions and intentions) separately and then combine them together to explain the action of digital piracy.

Body Paragraph

Consumers' ethical perceptions of piracy behavior will affect piracy action. According to Thongmak's (2017) article "Ethics, neutralization, and digital piracy", ethical perceptions are divided into two factors: morals (people with high moral standards) and neutralization (people who do not consider digital piracy a very harmful behavior). He also separates the piracy action into eight types and does multiple regression analysis to find the relationship between each perception and each piracy behavior (p.12). The results are shown in Table 1. Morals have negative influences on the first four types of actions in table 1, that is to say, people with higher ethical standards are less likely to download/buy & keep different types of digital goods (software, songs, movies and e-books), but the relations of moral and downloading/buying & sharing pirated goods are not significant. However, neutralization is a positive indicator of all types of piracy action (Thongmak, 2017), so people who do not take digital piracy seriously are more likely to download/buy & keep or share any types of digital products mentioned in the table. Therefore, purchasers' ethical perceptions, especially neutralization could lead to the pirating behavior of various digital products.

Consumers' ethical perceptions vary based on gender and downloader types. People of different genders have different perspectives of digital piracy and females are more likely to take it seriously. Thongmak (2017) calculates mean values and does t-tests for each ethical perception and piracy action in different groups: males and females (p.13). The results are shown in Table 2. The mean values of many items in Table 2 are almost the same in the two groups but the mean values of morals/ethics, download/buy & keep pirated software and download/buy & keep pirated movies for the female group are lower than those for the male group. Overall, females have higher moral standards and are less likely to pirate (download or buy and keep pirated software and movies) compared to males (Thongmak, 2017, p.13). In addition, the author states that heavy downloaders ("people who illegally buy or download digital products at least five times per month"(p.14)) have different neutralizations and morals compared with light downloaders ("people who pirate less than five times per month"(p.14)). Similarly, Thongmak (2017) determines mean values and does t-tests for each ethical perception and piracy action in the two groups (p.14-15), and the results are shown in Table 3. These results suggest that "There are between-group differences between heavy downloaders and light downloaders of all digital products in neutralization techniques and ethics except the ethics of heavy downloaders and light downloaders of e-books" (p.14), and that light downloaders own less neutralization and more ethics than heavy downloaders (p.14). It can be concluded that generally females or light downloaders are more virtuous than males or heavy downloaders respectively, and that light downloaders often take digital piracy more seriously than heavy downloaders do.

Consumers' intentions to purchase pirated digital goods is another major factor of pirating. Many scholars find similar results of intentions from their studies on digital piracy. By constructing a two-stage model and doing research on how intentions and willingness to pay (WTP) explain digital piracy, Jackman and Lorde (2013) calculate the ordinary least squares (OLS) estimates shown in panel 1 of Table 4 part (1). The authors find that the OLS estimate of intentions is 15.864 with three stars on the upper right in that table, and thus they indicate that "Intentions contribute significantly and positively to individuals' piracy behavior" (p.809). Also, Yoon (2011) indicates that in order to anticipate and learn more about particular pirating actions on specified occasions, Ajzen introduced a theory of planned behavior as an expansion of Fishbein and Ajzen's theory of reasoned action. Based on this theory, consumers' authentic piracy behavior is affected by their behavioral intents directly (cited in Yoon, 2011, p.406). In addition, Taylor (2012) uses self-report intentions in two studies and verifies that the relations of the information of intentions to pirate and pirating behavior are significant. Yoon (2011) even focuses only on the factor "consumers' intentions" and analyzes it in depth in order to find some approaches to predict digital piracy. Therefore, intentions to purchase unofficial digital products is a non-negligible determinant when searching for reasons of digital piracy.

Consumers' intentions can be influenced by many determinants, including ethical factors. Jackman and Lorde (2013) write the following equation to examine the factors of intentions to pirate:

$$Intentions = f\left(\underset{-}{attitudes,} \ \underset{-}{perceived\ consequences,} \ \underset{+}{relativism,} \ \underset{-}{education,} \ \underset{-}{facilitating\ conditions,} \ \underset{-}{age,} \ \underset{+/-}{gender} \right) \text{ (p.805)}$$

In this equation, intentions is a function of attitudes on piracy, perceived consequences of pirating action, relativism (a measure of ethics, "relativism measures a person's attitude towards universal moral principles and rules" (p.806)), education background, age and gender. The sign "+" under the factor represents that the determinant is a positive indicator of intentions, and the sign "-" under the factor shows that the determinant is a negative indicator of intentions, and "+/-" sign under the factor gender means that it is hard to determine whether gender is a positive indicator or a negative one. Then the authors do ordinary least squares (OLS) multiple regression, Tobit estimation and quantile regression analyses for the collected data, and the results are presented in Table 4 part (1) and part (2). The values of estimates and quantiles are very small in terms of gender and age, but those values of the other five factors listed in the table can not be ignored. Hence, consumers' pirating intentions could be affected by these five determinants, and thus Jackman and Lorde (2013) conclude that "Attitudes, perceived consequences, relativism, education and facilitating conditions had the largest impact on piracy intention in the proposed model" (p.814). In addition, the values of OLS estimates with respect to relativism, education and facilitating conditions are positive, so these three factors are positive predictors of intentions. On the contrary, the values of OLS estimates with respect to attitudes and perceived consequences are negative, which implies that these two determinants are negative predictors of intentions.

Also, Yoon (2011) uses an integrated model to combine the theory of planned behavior (TPB) and ethics theory to explain piracy intentions. According to the structural model and two behavioral theories, the author explores the relationship of intents to pirate and eight factors (subjective norm, attitude toward piracy, perceived behavioral control, moral obligation, justice, perceived benefit, perceived risk and habit) by determining the average variance extracted and correlation matrix and performing the hypothesis testing. The hypothesis testing results are shown in Table 5, and five conclusions can be made from these results. (1) The path coefficient from attitude toward piracy to intention to commit digital piracy is a positive number, so people who have a more positive attitude on piracy are more likely to have intentions to pirate. (2) The path coefficient from the moral obligation to intention to commit digital piracy is -0.57, a relatively large number in the table. Hence, the moral obligation has a straight and important influence on piracy intention (p.411), and people who have higher moral standards are less likely to have intents to pirate. (3) The values of path coefficient in rows H1 and H6 are positive and negative respectively, which suggests that justice is a negative predictor of piracy intentions. People who are more righteous and consider buying pirated products an unfair action are less willing to commit digital piracy. "In the social psychology literature, justice is considered equivalent to "equity"... Glass and Wood (1996) explain that people will perform an act of digital piracy and give the pirated products to others in exchange for social benefits" (p.413). In the "textbook" example mentioned in the introduction, when students think that purchasing piratic books is not unfair and that they can save more money by this piracy behavior, they might choose to go to the unofficial online store. (4) The values of path coefficient in rows H7 and H9 are positive and negative respectively, which implies that "Perceived benefits and perceived risk as perceived consequences of intended action have a significant impact on attitude toward digital piracy" (p.413). Since attitude is an important factor of piracy intentions, perceived consequences can not be ignored when analyzing intentions to commit digital piracy. (5) According to row H10, the path coefficient from habit to attitude toward piracy is 0.45, which is also a relatively large number in the table. Therefore, pirating habit has a comparatively essential influence on attitude toward digital piracy (p.414). To sum up, perceptions of justice, attitude toward digital piracy, perceived consequences of it and ethical or moral perceptions of it are the most important determinants of consumers' intentions to pirate.

Combining ethical perceptions, consumers' intentions and related factors together is important for explaining actual piracy behavior objectively. All these factors and their relations are shown in graph 1. In the graph, the moral obligation in Yoon's (2011) article and morals in Thongmak's (2017) article can be seen as the same concept because the explanations of them in each article are very similar. In addition, the factors with circles are less important than other factors. Also, it seems that justice or equity is similar to the ethical perceptions of digital piracy and that it is hard to determine whether justice can also be seen as a factor of ethical perceptions because people tend to use different concepts (like subjective norm and morals) of ethical perceptions in different articles. Unfortunately, the limited scope of this paper does not permit additional research on this topic.

Graph 1. Combining ethical perceptions, consumers' intentions for explaining digital piracy behavior

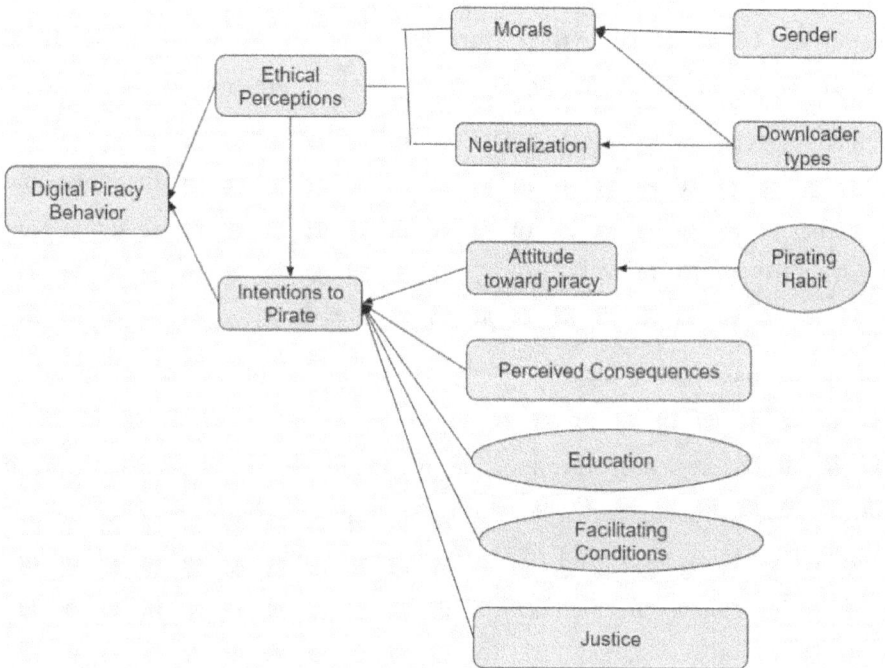

Self-report intentions and other surveys included in the sources mentioned above are valid. All the articles cited above use statistical tools like confirmatory factor analysis to show that their conclusions are reliable. Furthermore, Taylor (2012) specifically explores potential problems of the information of self-report digital piracy intentions in study 1. And he finds that the results agree with the hypothesis that the measurement of self-report intentions does not change related to different groups of gender, major, and grade-point average, and that "There is no identifiable evidence of threats to the results based upon issues related to common method variance (including social desirability bias) or sampling bias" (Taylor, 2012, p.474). Hence, the results used in this article are valid, and the statements concluded from these results are also reasonable.

According to the reasons for digital piracy, several possible strategies are proposed in the following paragraphs. Changing people's ethical perceptions of digital piracy might be one effective way to prevent piracy. Consumers' pirating action can be influenced by their neutralization or whether they consider digital piracy a very harmful behavior. Sisario (2011) indicates that the top Internet suppliers in the US have decided to classify purchasers suspicious of digital copyright piracy through an organized method and then warning them by e-mail or other ways. Then these Internet providers improve the alerting system, and Sisario (2011) states that "The system announced on Thursday involves a series of six warnings that an Internet provider can send to a customer whom the media companies have identified as a possible copyright infringe". The alert approaches expand from elementary e-mail warnings to a series of "mitigation measures" at levels 5 and 6 like decreased connecting speeds or Web browsing barriers (Sisario, 2011). The author agrees that lawsuits on such piracy behavior may be expensive and ineffective nowadays, and that this new warning method can be a substitution of litigation to make people take digital piracy more seriously. Milch also states that "This is a sensible approach to the problem of online content theft and, importantly, one that respects the privacy and rights of our subscribers" (cited in Sisario, 2011).

Hill (2007) offers two meaningful approaches to stop digital piracy with respect to justice or equity in the article "Digital Piracy: Causes, consequences, and strategic responses". One method is to separate the market and use different prices. Purchasers with lower income have the largest possibility to incur the thoughts of injustice and then buy piratic products, so the copyright holder ought to provide a low priced limited version goods to satisfy the demand of these people (p.20). When official stores sell limited functionality goods at prices similar to those of piratic goods, people may consider buying official products a more valuable action. Another method is "offering consumers who purchase the legitimate product something extra" (p.21). Hill (2007) indicates that computer software suppliers can "provide online services, such as periodic upgrades and security patches, to consumers who register the legal product using a security code that is unique to every legal copy of the product" (p.21). Consumers may find it fairer to purchase legitimate goods when they can obtain some extra benefits.

I also provide some general strategies to avoid digital piracy based on the factors of pirating action. Firstly, since attitude toward digital piracy affects intentions to pirate, our government and schools can propagandize more and even give some lectures on digital piracy, so that citizens would know more about its negative influences and the proper ways to buy and use digital products. The second strategy is that people's perceived consequences of digital piracy can be changed if our government perfects related law system, makes the law system more efficient, and punishes people who commit digital piracy. Then consumers' intentions to pirate would not be as strong as before. Finally, we need to pay more attention to students' ethical aspects in education. We ought to inform students of moral obligations and teach them to tell right from wrong. Helping students to develop a correct ethical perception is very important for weakening the pirating intentions as well as reducing digital piracy behaviors.

Conclusion

Consumers' ethical perspectives on buying pirated digital products can help predict digital piracy action, and it is also affected by gender and downloader types. Purchasers' intentions to pirate is another major factor of committing digital piracy, and the main determinants to explain why they have such (strong) intentions are their perceptions of justice, attitude toward digital piracy, perceived consequences of it and ethical or moral perceptions on it. Therefore, ethical perceptions and intentions are two determinants of digital piracy, and it is important to combine them and other related factors together in order to give an objective prediction of digital piracy behavior.

There are several possible strategies to avoid digital piracy based on the analyses of the determinants of digital piracy. One solution is to send warning messages to consumers who commit digital piracy so as to change their moral points of view on piracy. Another method is to reduce the perceptions of justice or inequity by selling limited functionality products at a lower price or giving additional benefits for people who purchase legal products. Furthermore, I previously provided three general strategies (propagandizing on negative influences of digital piracy and how to buy and use digital products, perfecting related law system and focusing more on students' ethical education) in terms of the factors attitude toward digital piracy, perceived consequences of it and moral perceptions of it respectively. Carrying out strategies similar to those mentioned above is necessary for countering digital piracy.

References

Hill, C. W. L. (2007). Digital piracy: Causes, consequences, and strategic responses. *APJM: Asia Pacific Journal of Management*, 24(1), 9-25. doi:http://dx.doi.org.proxy.lib.umich.edu/10.1007/s10490-006-9025-0

Jackman, M., & Lorde, T. (2014). Why buy when we can pirate? The role of intentions and willingness to pay in predicting piracy behavior. *International Journal of Social Economics*, 41(9), 801-819. doi:http://dx.doi.org.proxy.lib.umich.edu/10.1108/IJSE-04-2013-0104

Sisario, B. (2011). To Slow Piracy, internet providers ready penalties. *The New York Times*. Retrieved from https://www.nytimes.com/2011/07/08/technology/to-slow-piracy-internet-providers-ready-penalties.html

Taylor, S. A. (2012). Evaluating digital piracy intentions on behaviors. *The Journal of Services Marketing*, 26(7), 472-483. doi:http://dx.doi.org.proxy.lib.umich.edu/10.1108/08876041211266404

Thongmak, M. (2017). Ethics, neutralization, and digital piracy. *International Journal of Electronic Commerce Studies*, 8(1), 1-24. doi:http://dx.doi.org.proxy.lib.umich.edu/10.7903/ijecs.1436

Yoon, C. (2011). Theory of planned behavior and ethics theory in digital piracy: An integrated model. *Journal of Business Ethics*, 100(3), 405-417. Retrieved from https://proxy.lib.umich.edu/login?url= https://search-proquest-com.proxy.lib.umich.edu/ docview/902073691?accountid=14667

Appendix

Table 1. Results of multilinear regression analysis and hypotheses tests on ethical perceptions

(Thongmak, 2017, p.12)

Description	B	Beta
Neutralization → Download/buy & keep pirated software	.211	.201
Morals/ethics → Download/buy & keep pirated software	-.321	-.306
Neutralization → Download/buy & keep pirated songs	.364	.289
Morals/ethics → Download/buy & keep pirated songs	-.350	-.278
Neutralization → Download/buy & keep pirated movies	.223	.186
Morals/ethics → Download/buy & keep pirated movies	-.279	-.232
Neutralization → Download/buy & keep pirated e-books	.270	.255
Morals/ethics → Download/buy & keep pirated e-books	-.070	-.067
Neutralization → Download/buy & share pirated software	.195	.230
Morals/ethics → Download/buy & share pirated software	-.088	-.104
Neutralization → Download/buy & share pirated songs	.366	.313
Morals/ethics → Download/buy & share pirated songs	-.162	-.138
Neutralization → Download/buy & share pirated movies	.239	.254
Morals/ethics → Download/buy & share pirated movies	-.092	-.098
Neutralization → Download/buy & share pirated e-books	.235	.271
Morals/ethics → Download/buy & share pirated e-books	-.020	-.023

$< .05$, $**p$-value $< .01$.

Table 2. T-test of group differences in means between females and males
(Thongmak, 2017, p.14)

Factor	Group	Mean	SD	t-value	p-value
Neutralization	Females	3.1624	.90577	-.239	.811
	Males	3.1880	.91399		
Morals/ethics	Females	3.0251	.87024	3.095	.002**
	Males	2.7179	.79222		
Download/buy & keep pirated software	Females	2.36	1.000	-3.136	.002**
	Males	2.74	1.092		
Download/buy & keep pirated songs	Females	3.18	1.242	.733	.464
	Males	3.07	1.291		
Download/buy & keep pirated movies	Females	2.46	1.101	-2.451	.015*
	Males	2.82	1.317		
Download/buy & keep pirated e-books	Females	3.18	1.242	.733	.464
	Males	3.07	1.291		
Download/buy & share pirated software	Females	1.57	.830	-1.137	.257
	Males	1.68	.877		
Download/buy & share pirated songs	Females	1.99	1.215	1.264	.207
	Males	1.82	1.08		
Download/buy & share pirated movies	Females	1.60	.915	-.629	.530
	Males	1.67	.983		
Download/buy & share pirated e-books	Females	1.37	.797	-.885	.377
	Males	1.46	.970		

Note: *p-value < .05, **p-value < .01.

Table 3. T-test of group differences in means between heavy downloaders and light downloaders
(Thongmak, 2017, p.15)

Factor	Group	Mean	SD	t-value	p-value
Neutralization	Heavy downloaders (Software)	3.4548	.78122	4.663	.000**
	Light downloaders (Software)	2.9765	.93887		
Morals/ethics	Heavy downloaders (Software)	2.6156	.85015	-5.146	.000**
	Light downloaders (Software)	3.1080	.79684		
Neutralization	Heavy downloaders (Songs)	3.3608	.85059	5.214	.000**
	Light downloaders (Songs)	2.8115	.90771		
Morals/ethics	Heavy downloaders (Songs)	2.7705	.84244	-3.929	.000**
	Light downloaders (Songs)	3.1667	.81517		
Neutralization	Heavy downloaders (Movies)	3.3521	.83025	3.292	.001**
	Light downloaders (Movies)	3.0137	.94502		
Morals/ethics	Heavy downloaders (Movies)	2.7136	.80737	-3.777	.000**
	Light downloaders (Movies)	3.0766	.85817		
Neutralization	Heavy downloaders (E-books)	3.5860	.72591	4.525	.000**
	Light downloaders (E-books)	3.0764	.91963		
Morals/ethics	Heavy downloaders (E-books)	2.7544	.86264	-1.497	.135
	Light downloaders (E-books)	2.9417	.84850		

Note: *p-value < .05, **p-value < .01.

Table 4. Empirical results of intentions and willingness to pay (1)
(Jackman and Lorde, 2013, p.810)

Table 4. Empirical results of intentions and willingness to pay (2)
(Jackman and Lorde, 2013, p.810)

	OLS estimates	Tobit estimates	25th quantile	50th quantile	75th quantile
Panel 1: determinants of actual piracy					
Intentions	15.864***(1.590)	19.917***(2.042)	23.519***(1.692)	12.943***(1.467)	3.181***(0.675)
Willingness to pay	−0.290***(0.063)	−0.442***(0.079)	−0.248***(0.055)	−0.467***(0.052)	−0.182***(0.022)
Panel 2: determinants of piracy intentions					
Attitudes	−0.763***(0.104)	n.a.	−0.988***(0.135)	−0.898***(0.121)	−0.721***(0.104)
Perceived consequences	−0.079***(0.022)	n.a.	0.181(0.158)	−0.322***(0.075)	−0.256***(0.052)
Ethics – relativism	0.408***(0.108)	n.a.	0.096***(0.029)	0.096***(0.025)	0.104***(0.019)
Education	0.071*(0.040)	n.a.	0.438***(0.136)	0.340***(0.115)	0.407***(0.094)
Facilitating conditions	0.278**(0.139)	n.a.	0.038(0.055)	0.063(0.045)	0.025(0.036)
Gender	−0.100(0.120)	n.a.	−0.099(0.158)	0.035(0.138)	−0.034(0.113)
Age	−0.006(0.004)	n.a.	−0.003(0.005)	−0.010**(0.005)	−0.012***(0.004)
Panel 3: determinants of willingness to pay					
Income	0.001(0.001)	0.001(0.001)	0.002**(0.001)	0.002***(0.001)	0.001(0.001)
Perceived importance	13.772***(3.271)	13.532***(3.340)	7.345**(3.067)	9.309***(2.558)	21.859***(3.697)
Moral judgment – idealism	3.284(3.364)	3.597(3.486)	2.322(1.647)	6.274***(1.510)	3.722**(1.540)
Facilitating conditions	−5.836***(2.207)	−5.932***(2.242)	−7.557**(3.321)	−0.712(2.648)	−0.339(3.550)
Gender	−4.025(4.455)	−4.146(4.548)	1.659(3.491)	3.471(2.845)	−5.273(4.044)
Age	0.077(0.206)	0.050(0.210)	0.125(0.117)	0.063(0.099)	−0.167(0.147)

Notes: ***,**,*Represents statistical significance at the 1, 5 and 10 per cent levels of testing, respectively. SE are in parentheses

Table 5. Hypothesis testing results on ethical theories
(Yoon, 2011, p.414)

Hypothesis	Path	Path coefficient	t value	Result
H1	Subjective norm → Intention to commit digital piracy	0.18	3.36	**
H2	Attitude toward piracy → Intention to commit digital piracy	0.12	2.34	**
H3	Perceived behavioral control → Intention to commit digital piracy	0.23	4.28	**
H4	Moral obligation → Intention to commit digital piracy	−0.57	12.18	**
H5	Moral obligation → Subjective norm	−0.28	5.43	**
H6	Justice → Subjective Norm	−0.09	1.76	*
H7	Perceived benefit → Attitude toward piracy	0.10	1.67	*
H8	Perceived benefit → Intention to commit digital piracy	0.20	3.98	**
H9	Perceived risk → Attitude toward piracy	−0.20	3.74	**
H10	Habit → Attitude toward piracy	0.45	7.92	**

Subjective norm R^2: 0.391.
Attitude toward piracy R^2: 0.351.
Intention to commit digital piracy R^2: 0.519.
*Significant at the 0.05 level, **significant at the 0.01 level.

Excellence in Multilingual Writing

Do Not Take Anything Slightly
by Kyungrae Lee
From WRITING 120
Nominated by Scott Beal

Kyungrae Lee's essay candidly examines the factors, both external and internal, that led to his descent from being a highly-reputed student at the University of Wisconsin to landing on academic probation at the University of Michigan. One of the highlights of Kyungrae's colorful and clear voice is the way he levels with the reader directly, using metacommentary effectively to shape our understanding of why he is telling his story and what one might learn from it.

-- Scott Beal

Do Not Take Anything Slightly

In this essay, I am going to tell my personal story. I want you to be patient with me. The story starts when I first arrived here in University of Michigan winter 2018. I was full of confidence and I thought I could do whatever I could. Indeed, I was a good student in Korea and at the University of Wisconsin where I transferred from. I thought I could easily break the language barrier down when I encountered it. Also, I thought I was good at time management skills. Of course, I thought I could smoothly deal with schoolwork as well. However, none of the things above I mentioned succeeded after I came here to the U of M. I did not do things with the sense of responsibility and acknowledge my inability to complete schoolwork in limited time. I overestimated myself. Everything I had imagined was my delusions after all. Everything was completely different from what I expected such as workloads, social interactions with other students – even with professors. There is more volume of reading and writing than I had thought of. I could not even keep up with my study. Lack in English skills made me more nervous. This led me to take much longer time than average students here in the University of Michigan. I will talk about more about what I experienced later. In any case, I failed at the very first semester since I transferred from Wisconsin to here. If I had done things seriously and prepared beforehand, I would have not gotten low grades and would not be on special probation because of low GPA in Fall 2019. This is all because I saw everything green in my eye.

In Korea, there is a unique and well-known fable regarding a small frog. The main character, a frog, in this fable is so similar to my situation. Let me give you a short explanation of the story. While he is living in a deep well, the frog is satisfied to see the limited sky given to him even though he cannot climb up the wall of the well. He does not have to consider serious things happening outside because he has always been in his safe zone. Also, food keeps coming in from the outside of the well continuously. No one cares what is inside in the dark well, so he could stay there safe for a long time. The point of this story is that he really does not know what will happen to him after the well does not sustain him any longer. The wall might cave in and he might be short of food supply. What is he supposed to do in this case? He will never know what he should do because he has never gone through those incidents. He, the frog, should have tried to climb the wall right in front of him. This fable reflected my current circumstances that I faced. I thought I had enough experiences to cope with challenges, but those experiences were not enough at all.

This fable links me to my personal story in Korea until I came to U.S. and Wisconsin in 2017. Those places were my safe zones. When I was in university in Korea, I was highly appreciated by professors and students near me. One of the professors, who once the vice-minister of Labor Department in my country, said I talked like a doctor when I gave presentations in front of whole class and the professor. My experience in the Navy was unique as well. For all men in Korea it has always been mandatory to serve the country via joining the armed forces. Ninety percent of men usually choose to go to Army, but rather I chose to go into Navy and selected as informant collecting information from North Korea's army. I was so proud of myself to being in part of this huge and important organization. In 2017 at the University of Wisconsin, I was there for two semester as somewhat of an exchange student. Professors there praised for my progress and abilities that I showed. But at that time, I wanted more beyond the current situation. I thought I am the person who can do more without difficulties. I also wanted academic reputation, honor, and to get a higher level of education. Therefore, I chose to transfer to U of M. I took actions right after I made the decision. I could receive many recommendation letters within one semester at the University of Wisconsin. Those achievements made me more arrogant. I always knew that carelessness is the root of all evil, but I did not seriously recognize this fact deep in my subconsciousness. Or maybe I was too conscious of others.

I am not trying to show off what I have accomplished and done until now. You, my essay reader, also achieved a lot in your life. You got admitted getting into this school, I know. I did not know what you have done so far, but I heard from others, their stories before they came here. For example, one of my roommates can speak more than four languages naturally and friends here were elected the president of the student council. I met "Rossholes" (Ross business school students plus asshole) in person and they spoke to me implicitly why they are so great. Moreover, most of the international students I am faced with graduated from boarding schools or high schools in the U.S. Or, they have spent many years in the U.S., so they are so familiar with using English. When I saw them speaking English fluently, I felt a sense of shame on me. Even if I heard that I could speak well by my American friends, it was solely their point of view which saw me as a foreigner. In real settings, including both everyday life and in-class situations, I may look like a kid mumbling to someone. Except what I have experienced, there would be more stories I could not even imagine. I thought I was a mere small frog once again. Comparisons with others made me feel small. Unlike while I was in Wisconsin, I could not communicate deeply. The comparisons did not help me to communicate with peers in class and professors. I should have admitted my current circumstances, but I could not admit my reality because I was the frog in the deep. I had to realize that I was just as the frog who did not want to get out of the deep well.

While I was in University of Wisconsin in 2017, there were not so many courses demanding of me teamwork or discussions. I did not have many chances to face with other native speakers. Also, the level of learning material was not high enough to bring me to the utmost limit of my ability. In Michigan, however, there are many in-class discussion and teamwork, which is mandatory in here. I could not say what I want to say exactly due to high level of concepts used in class, so I dragged the time in class when I had to have conversation with peers. I felt frustrated seeing the face of other peers stuffy. The sweat came out every day. When I had to do peer-reviews for instance, I felt guilty all the time about my work because my peers could not get enough feedback merely because of me. I could see their face that did not expect anything of me. This was the same in math115 class. During teamwork assignments, I had to understand the problems and solve them with peers, but I was an observer not doing anything. I could not understand what the problem asked of me. In addition, while listening to lecture, I often could not follow what the main point is. The details about the lecture is no need to mention as well. When professors used academic jargon, slang, or common sense which is widely spread throughout North America, I became deaf. So, I tried to use office hours and contact with professors to deal with the issues as often as possible, but I could not even understand what the professor said to me when I met him or her face to face. I could not tell what I was trying to say exactly as well. I could see them feel stuffy too! Horrible experiences did not end with those things.

Reading and writing were one of the biggest issues as well. All the activities during the lecture begin with a proper reading of the course material. As you might expect, I could not properly read the course material. If I were in Korea, I could easily read more than thirty pages in a day. Also, while in the University of Wisconsin, I did not have to read as much volume as here to write two- or three-page length of paper. Here the materials that I have to read are about thirty to fifty pages per essay and the content is more difficult than that of University of Wisconsin covered. When reading seven or eight pages of a text, it took three or four times of hours for me to read than others and I was not sure if I understood the main points correctly. Translation was the main problem. Facing with foreign language first, I had to translate in my own native language. Then, I have to understand literal meaning of it. Finally, I have to understand the implicit meaning. For example, it was required for me to see what is behind the face value of a product. Because in economics terms, the price of one product not only reflect suppliers' cost but customer's demand. Overall it shows the value of the product. Back to the point, I had to keep challenging myself in lectures and discussions. Difficulties continued in writing. Without concrete understanding of the reading, how could well-established essay or report can be written? Without concrete understanding of the reading, I could not communicate with my essay readers, which means writing was not meaningful to both of us. Think, when you have to make an argument even when you did not understand the subject enough. Proper word choice, grammar, sentence building, structuring, argument, and counterargument did not matter if I misunderstood the whole reading. I thought my English skills will improve as time goes on. I believed. I lost my faith after going through the suffering moment which lasted for two months. I gave up. Time management could not be something to say when I could not properly deal with English after all.

Balance, I have always wanted, between life and school was trampled by a giant symbolized as language barriers. I had to study political science class materials until 4 a.m. to take a quiz and prepare for math class. These processes were continued for two months until I gave up. I slept three or four hours a day to catch up with my enrolled courses. My physical and mental health became so bad. Perception of time became obscure to me because I had always needed to deal with the issues ahead of me. Doing so, I could not get up early and attend class on time. I thought I could not live like this, so I chose school rather than socializing with other people. My social relationships with other Koreans were collapsed. I could not participate in the club activities in which I was interested such as fencing and basketball. I failed in everything. My impression about the first semester in this university was very awful. As nobody intends to make one's life stressful or miserable, I did try my best, but my first semester in this school was tough. Eventually, now I am on special probation for low grades. I still have to deal with the unresolved courses from previous 2018 winter semester. Back to the fable, the wall the frog faced was so slippery for him to climb up. At that time, he lost his confidence and gave up when the wall of the well sunk.

Some might say that I did not adapt to circumstances since I came here in the U of M, and I still do not. Yes. I truly admitted. In my first semester, 2018 winter semester, here after transferring from University of Wisconsin, I was so self-conscious when others watched me. I did not do the right thing. I hung out with friends many times, not studying at all sometimes. Even when the test date was three days away. I drank alcohol many times, not caring about myself.

I took everything lightly. When it comes to thinking about what I had done as social activities, however, I put my effort in forming my group to help me to adapt here and feel a sense of belonging into this place. I thought studying was not only an important thing but also maintaining social relationships with others were significant. By doing so, though, it was significantly tough for me to finish the large volume of readings and many undone assignments after mingling with friends. Every time I went to class, assignments were "assigned" to me. I had to read more than twenty pages to take daily quiz and write two to three-page long response paper for each course. I was taking Math 115, English 124, Polsci 115, and EECS 183 courses then. Every class required me to spend three hours per course a day. I could not endure the workload. I thought I might not the right person to study here. Other students and friends near me deemed to do well on their work. I felt a sense of shame on me. I should not have compared myself with others, but I did. I gave up in the middle of the winter semester just as I said above. At last, I took a year off. It was my restoration time to stand up again and move ahead. Even coming back here now, I am still immature, but I am trying to do my best at least my viewpoint. Anyone who feel the same as me let's not give up. We have promising future ahead of us, I believe.

I may not qualify to give you recommendations what you need to do here. I just want to share my experiences through my essay and do not want you to follow my steps. Before we go back to our countries again and work there or go into bigger world, we all want to make good memories here in this university. Time will never go back as you know. It keeps flowing all the time no matter how you yell at it. All I want for you is not looking down on anything in here. You and I will confront more difficulties in here and afterward. Since we are not natives in the U.S., we cannot be welcomed by others if we are not ready. I, the frog, am struggling to deal with issues from the last semester and current courses. I am trying my best to climb up the wall of the deep well as long as I can. While climbing up the wall, the bird might mock at you or pass over you. Do not be swayed by others. You cannot be a bird, natives might be the case in your circumstance, flying high up above the wall in the well. You have to believe your own strength: perseverance. This attitude come about by not seeing something merely in your perspective; Do not look down on courses you are taking, for example. Do not be arrogant until the last minute!

Excellence in the Practice of Writing

黄瑞欣 "Huángruìxīn"

by Alyssa Huang
From WRITING 100: The Practice of Writing
Nominated by Gina Brandolino

In this deeply moving essay, Alyssa builds upon the course materials we studied as we considered our course theme of "Monsters" to explore the feelings of isolation and alienation she experienced as an Asian-American who often felt, as she says, "caught in a tug-of-war between two cultures . . . and at risk of being shunned by the societies of each." She bravely describes situations in which her "more Asian" friends make her feel--or even call her--"white-washed" and how terrible that feels. And at the lovely conclusion of this essay, we see Alyssa making regular visits to her grandparents' house, learning to cook Chinese cuisine, no longer feeling like such an outsider.

-- Gina Brandolino

黄瑞欣 "Huángruìxīn"

Sensing a presence nearby, I look up from my sketchbook. Standing in front of me is a woman dressed in a large purple coat and black gloves, even though we're inside in the Art and Architecture Building. She's probably in her late sixties or early seventies, but it's hard to fully tell with her big black sunglasses covering the upper part of her face. She's smiling kindly at me, and I suddenly feel a slight sense of nostalgia.

"你说中文吗？" she asks me ("Do you speak Chinese?").

Hesitantly, I reply, "对一点点." (Yes, a little).

"------- 旅游 ？"

I freeze up. Just as I regretfully predicted, the woman proceeds to ask a question that I can't answer.

"什么？对不起…" (What? Sorry…)

"------- 旅游 ？" Patiently, she says it slower this time.

I can make out some words like "旅游"; she's asking how to get somewhere. But my Chinese isn't advanced enough to decipher exactly where she wants to go.

"Ah, 我不懂, 对不起," (I don't understand, I'm sorry) I say apologetically.

"Oh, 你不懂," she echoes back and nods, "没关系." (It's okay).

As she walks away, I can feel my insides coiling in disappointment in myself. I've seen plenty of older Asian women with her appearance where I grew up in San Jose, California: a full head of permed hair that's dyed jet black, clothes that cover the majority of their body from the sun, sizeable, dark sunglasses, lips that are decorated with a dusty pink lipstick. But for some reason in particular, this woman reminded me of my two grandmothers.

As children, both sets of my grandparents immigrated with their families from their home countries to the US to start better lives. On my mom's side, my grandparents came from mainland China, and on my dad's side, they came from Taiwan, taking their cultures and traditions with them. They grew up, married, had children, and then grandchildren all in the US, designating me, my brother, and cousins, as third generation Chinese and Taiwanese-born Americans. As each generation was brought up in America, we gradually became more and more disconnected from our Chinese and Taiwanese roots. As a third generation, I can barely speak my native languages, remember the specific dates of traditional holidays, and display mannerisms that are commonly held in China and Taiwan. On top of that, by growing up in the Bay Area where many people my age are second generation, my friends would tease me for being unexpectedly more ignorant of my culture. Not being able to assist the woman in the Art and Architecture Building evoked and worsened my already self-conscious guilt that I had let down my relatives and deep-rooted heritage by submitting myself to being "Americanized" and too white-washed. Meanwhile, to other Americans of different backgrounds, I am simply how I appear: Asian. Similar to the wolf girls' experiences in "St. Lucy's Home for Girls Raised by Wolves," both they and I are caught in a tug of war between two cultures we grew up around, and at risk of being shunned by the societies of each. For this reason, both of us are considered monsters.

When I was five, my parents signed me up for Chinese school. Every week, my brother and I and about ten other children went to a woman's house in our neighborhood where she taught all of us Mandarin. She was in her forties with glasses and short hair, and she had converted her whole family room into a makeshift classroom with desks and chairs with our Chinese names on them. We called her *Lǐ lǎoshī*, which is Chinese for Teacher Li. Generally, I don't have many memories of Chinese school at all -- just small, irrelevant fragments of playing with old friends during breaktime, struggling to write characters by the correct stroke order, watching a boy argue with *Lǐ lǎoshī* over how a question mark is written, and singing the song "*Xiǎo fēijī*," or "Little Airplane," over and over. Despite my lack of recollection however, my Chinese name that my parents chose for me, *Huángruìxīn* (黄瑞欣), remained permanently etched in my mind after hearing *Lǐ lǎoshī* address me by it so many times, and writing it repeatedly on my homework assignments. I continued to attend Chinese school as I grew older, but eventually we couldn't fit it into my schedule anymore and I had to be withdrawn from the program. After countless years of failing to learn online, and neglecting practice with my parents and grandparents, I began to forget what I had picked up, until I'd forgotten almost everything entirely.

Claudette recounts a similar experience when describing the results of her training at St. Lucy's in "St. Lucy's Home for Girls Raised by Wolves". Once her assimilation to human civilization was complete, Claudette had forgotten the layout of the woods she used to be so familiar with, and ultimately the memories of her past life. When she was given special permission by the nuns to visit her family in the woods, Claudette had to be accompanied by a woodsman, as she admitted "[she] couldn't remember how to find the way back on [her] own"(339). The wolf girl's schooling at St. Lucy's transformed them entirely with respect to their mannerisms, language, and perspectives toward their previous and new ways of life. Similar to how Claudette and her sisters completed their training at St. Lucy's and lost all traces of their wolflike nature by the end of the story, I was unable to continue learning Mandarin, and as a result, lost a potential bond to my heritage. Additionally, by breaking off from learning Chinese, I had taken a step farther away from my ethnicity, and a step closer to a version of myself that I didn't want to become. Mirroring how Claudette describes feeling immense sadness when she visited her family by the end, my own negligence to pick up Chinese again and restore myself within my roots would become one of my biggest regrets in the future. Both the wolf girls and I were raised to conform to two different societies and are now stuck in a cultural purgatory as a consequence. This state of ambiguity would breed many more troubles for me in the future.

I hopped onto the bed, my childish demeanor delighting in the mattress's bounce. My cousin, Emily, flopped down on it beside me, rolling onto her stomach. She's followed by our friend, Izzy (who is Caucasian), who we became close with at a dance studio we all used to go to. All three of us are the same age, and we often spent time at each other's houses. We talked comfortably for a while on Izzy's bed about random things children are prone to discuss -- at one point, one of us brought up the topic of places we've visited. A knocking on the door briefly interrupted our excited exchange on Disneyworld and Hawaii, and Izzy's older sister, Julia, and her friend (who is also Caucasian) entered the room. They both sat cross-legged on the carpet, and we continued our conversation. The talk was enjoyable for some time, and then I remembered that during the past summer, Emily and I visited Beijing and Shanghai with our families and grandparents. We went inside the Bird Nest where they held the 2008 Olympics, ate delicious food, and visited famous temples and night markets. I decided to bring it up, hoping Emily and I could share our adventures. "Emily and I went to China before," I declared eagerly. Instead, to my silent surprise, I was met with cold reticence. To break the tension, I hastily added "It was really fun." Julia's friend was the first to speak up.

"Oh, I'm learning about China in school right now," she remarked indifferently. But then she shook her head, locked her eyes on mine for a brief moment, and sighed. "Nothing over there but communists." Her tone was judgmental and snobby, and I could feel a mixture of confusion and anger well up inside of me (*Can she not tell Emily and I have a Chinese heritage? Or does she just not care if she offends us?*). Even as a child I was aware of China's history, but I still felt pride for our culture, especially after our visit. I quickly scrambled to defend myself.

"China's not that bad," I said cautiously, and I looked towards Emily for support. And maybe it's because she wanted to impress the older people in the room, or maybe it's because they were of another race, but to my surprise, she did the opposite.

"I *hate* China!" she exclaimed, a sort of half-smile creeping up onto her face. "There's a ton of pollution, everybody wears *gray* for some reason -- China sucks!"

"How could you say that?!" I shot back discreetly, "*We're* Chinese!" Detecting the exaggeration in her statements, and having known Emily all my life, I knew she didn't really stand by her claims. Besides, we were by each other's sides the entire trip, and I knew she had as much fun as I did. Regardless, all at once I felt victimized by her pretending to resent being Chinese, and by Julia's friend passive-aggressively generalizing China to solely a communist country. I wanted to stand by my assertions and be proud of my cultural identity, but at the same time I wanted to run out of the room out of pain of feeling like I didn't belong.

Comparable to how I felt rejected by Julia's friend's words and threatened by the pressure of being a person of color in a Caucasian-dominated society, Claudette details an identical scenario when she was caught and punished for not feeding the ducks and allowing Mirabella to prowl independently and strangle the wildlife in the duck pond. As a consequence, the nuns forced Claudette to watch a slideshow warning her of what would happen if she failed to finish her instruction at St. Lucy's. She describes the slides as displaying wolf girls who had been cast out of the home and had attempted to either rejoin their wolf packs or enter human society, but were ultimately viewed by the others with disdain for being different. The final slide contained the words, "Do you want to end up shunned by both species?"(332). The nuns encouraged that all the girls become adjusted to human lifestyles so that they can be accepted into human society, for they recognized that the wolf girls were stuck between two cultural identities, and advocated that they choose one and stick to it, or else they would be dismissed by both. Correspondingly, I was caught in a situation in which I was conflicted on whether to pretend to be more Caucasian (like my cousin, whose actions were similar to many other Asian Americans who feel they must act in such a way to survive in a more Caucasian-dominant environment), or to defend my ethnicity. Either way, I felt like a monster who could not entirely belong in any community.

It was senior year, and the bell rang to signal the end of fourth period and the start of lunch. I packed up my backpack and headed out to meet my friends at our usual spot by the benches next to the bike racks. As I approached the area, I could already see two of them, Joyce and Adrian, both second generation

Asian Americans. They were standing side by side, and Joyce was showing him something on her phone and giggling. "Hey guys," I said with a hint of curiosity, taking off my backpack, "What's so funny?"

Joyce looked up at me. "Uh, it's a post on 'Subtle Asian Traits,'" she responded. I was already familiar with the Twitter page that posts memes most Asian Americans can relate to.

I asked, "Can I see it too?"

Joyce shifted her weight half-grudgingly, "Well I can show it to you, but you need to know Chinese to get the joke, and since you're more white-washed…" her voice died down, almost as if she regretted saying the words as they came out of her mouth. Upon hearing them, I got irritated immediately. Even Adrian didn't make any effort to hide his shock at Joyce's words. Being called "white-washed" or "Americanized" by another Asian feels almost as offensive and derogatory as any racial slur. Although I sometimes used those words ironically to describe myself, I didn't expect someone else to call me by them seriously.

"*What?* Wow." I huffed.

Joyce stuttered to save herself, "But it's true!" she insisted. "Here, you can see it." She showed me her phone, and I looked at the post, silently predicting that my chances of proving her wrong were already slim. As I anticipated, the post was entirely in Chinese, and I could only pick out a few characters that I recognized.

"Yeah, I can't read it," I muttered, attempting to hide my dejection.

"Yeah, see, you wouldn't get it." Joyce affirmed dismissively. The dynamic between Asian Americans of different generations can be complex and frustrating. Being the only third generation in my friend group of second generation Asian-Americans, I endured the pressure of being disconnected from my culture more than ever. I'm not fluent in Chinese, although many people, including my friends, expect me to be -- and I caught many of them resenting me for that in the past.

Just as I've been labelled as an outsider by other Asian Americans, Claudette and her family were in a similar position before she and her sisters were taken to St. Lucy's. She details how her parents "ostracized the local wolves by having sometimes-thumbs, and regrets, and human children"(326). Being werewolves, Claudette's parents did not fit in with neither local wolves nor humans, as they physically transitioned between both regularly. When they had human children, they subsequently put them in the same situation. The wolf girls did not ask to be born as offspring of werewolves, and I did not ask to be born third generation, which made me not "Asian" enough to connect as well with first or second generation Asian Americans, but at the same time not "white-washed" enough to connect with other Americans either. Regardless, we were still resented by the societies we were brought up in due to our lifestyles being noncommittal to both, not fully belonging to any culture but our own intermingled one. It wasn't until recently when I began to cultivate an acceptance towards my background.

My grandparents on my mom's side live just five minutes away from us. When my brother and I were younger, they would pick us up after school and we would spend our time at their house until either our mom or dad came back from work. Once my brother was old enough to drive, however, we were able to go straight home every day, and visits to our grandparents' became less and less frequent. This continued until my senior year class schedule worked out so I had sixth period off, so every Wednesday and Friday I got out at 12:30 pm because my high school went by block scheduling. On the first Friday of the school year, I received a text from my mom asking me to relay a package from our house to my grandparents. After school I drove home, picked up the package, and drove to their house. Planning to briefly stop by, say hi, and drop off the package, I promptly knocked on their door. My grandpa answered it, a typical tired-looking, but lovable old man with graying hair and square glasses.

"Hi Y-kong!" I said, smiling. Technically, he should be addressed as Y-kon, but when we were small my cousins and brother and I called him "Y-kong" by accident, and we've called him that ever since, not bothering to change.

"*Ah-lee-sah-sah*," Y-kong said happily, calling me by a baby version of my name translated to Chinese pinyin. We hug, and I hand him the package. "Ah, thank you," he said, inspecting it. "Do you want to come inside? Y-poa and I are having lunch." Unable to refuse the offer, I followed him in and was welcomed by the familiar scent of aging wood, dried fruit, and the ever-present aroma of leftovers. My grandma, a stout woman with a bright round face, was sitting on their dark red couch watching TV, surrounded by pillows and snacks. The TV was turned on to a familiar Chinese news broadcast. After spending countless years at my grandparents' house after school and hearing it constantly in the background as I did my homework, I could still recognize the same introduction that played before the news anchor began chattering in Mandarin.

"Is that *Ah-lee-sah*?" Y-poa turned around to look at me. She smiled, got up from the couch, and hugged me. Y-kong made me a sandwich and the three of us sat together on the couch, talked, and watched the news. Both of them were very happy to hear that I was out of school so early on Fridays. After that day, we agreed that every Friday I could come over for lunch and spend time with them. They taught me how to cook too, and as a result I learned to prepare innumerable Chinese dishes. Food had become the newly discovered bridge to my culture from these experiences. I learned to cook rice cakes with pork, pig feet, eggs with tomato and green onions, steamed sweet potatoes, shrimp with black sesame garlic sauce, Chinese sausage with vegetables, salt and pepper duck, and the list goes on. I loved when we would sit together after cooking and talk and eat, my grandparents chatting to each other in Chinese every so often, and me still trying to consciously translate to myself what they were saying. After lunch, we would sit on the couch and watch the usual Chinese news station or political show. I would stare confusedly at the Mandarin subtitles flashing endlessly at the bottom of the screen, trying to connect the words I was hearing to the characters, and the characters I was looking at to English -- but most of the time I would have to ask Y-poa or Y-kong to translate, which they always did with a kind understanding.

"It's okay," Y-poa would say, "I don't expect you to know what they're talking about. This kind of political talk is very advanced anyway." But instead of feeling reassured, I felt more worried than ever. What if I visited China or Taiwan again, and they weren't there to help translate for me? What if my parents weren't there either? I knew at some point it would be possible. Even larger questions loomed over me during this time. What if I never remember when Chinese New Year is? Or the Mid-Autumn Festival? Will I still have to hand out red envelopes, or *hóngbāo* to children when I'm older? How much worse will my disconnection from my culture get? What if, when I'm older, I won't be able to find solace in any community at all? The uncertainty of my future as a third-generation Asian American caused discomfort for me throughout my life, and even made me feel freakish and despicable at times. But during my senior year, spending time with my grandparents lent an escape from it and helped me realize that I was enough. With them, none of it mattered. I was home, and I belonged.

Excellence in the Practice of Writing

I am a Twig in a Nature of Drawing:
The Story of Finding my Major
by Dallas Witbeck
From WRITING 100: The Practice of Writing
Nominated by Hannah Webster

"I am a Twig in a Nature of Drawing: The Story of Finding my Major" takes on feelings of being an impostor familiar to many first generation students. The central metaphor of the twig, pulled from the opening paragraph throughout the essay, is a unique and lovely way to consider the additional difficulties first generation students face when choosing a major. The writing is compelling and vivid.

-- Hannah Webster

I am a Twig in a Nature of Drawing: The Story of Finding my Major

I dream to be an architect someday. I didn't think I knew the first time I came to the University of Michigan campus. Caught in a mix of insecurity and apprehension, I ignored the obvious hints that the University itself was giving me. During the summer before my junior year of high school, I wasn't too focused on where I wanted to go to college. I figured I'd apply to some of the bigger colleges in Michigan and hope for the best. Even more distant in my mind was the question of majors, degrees, and types of classes. I was just focused on getting accepted somewhere so I could study something. My very first visit to the campus of the University of Michigan, before I became a student at the University, was stressed. My little brother was a patient at The C.S. Mott Children's Hospital for surgery. After multiple consultations it was the popular recommendation for him receive surgery in Ann Arbor to mend a bone deformity in his legs. The morning of his surgery was tense. After parking the car, my family and I walked towards double doors that belonged to the hospital. I didn't feel a particular obligation to pay any attention to the aesthetics of the hospital, but for one second I paused. When the doors opened, I was immediately struck with the awe of a unique art installation.

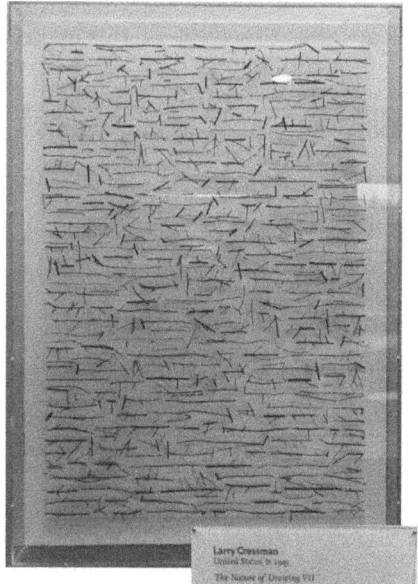

Larry Cressman
United States b 1946
The Nature of Drawing VII

The Nature of Drawing was the first thing I had seen at the University of Michigan that made me feel something indescribable. It was calming and inspiring, the first thing most patients saw when visiting the hospital. I couldn't explain my sudden need to desperately search for my phone camera to document my feelings. I remember that day, filled with worry for my brother, and I made a post on Instagram and captioned it "I appreciate this art." I felt a connection to the University through my love of this piece of art; when I recently revisited the hospital to see the Nature of Drawing VII again, I had the strong feelings. This time, the feelings were similar, inspiration, comfort, but also, this time I felt appreciative. Back when we left the hospital with my mended brother, I held a sort of admiration and fascination to the university. When I decided to apply first choice to the University of Michigan, I didn't think about the Nature of Drawing VII. But somehow the impression it created on my first experience at the University was peculiar. The campus became specifically alluring to me.

I cried when I got an email, an acceptance to UofM, in the spring of my senior year. I felt a lift, the relief of success, of hard work. Something about the University felt special to me. I do contain one characteristic I viewed as a setback. I am a first-generation college student. Generally, in the Universities eyes, being a first-generation student is an honor, and I had always felt a responsibility to be the first in my family to attend university. The UMich webpage supports and encourages first generation students and states students view a "college degree as changing future possibilities not just for an individual, but for a whole family." and "First generation college students pave the way and create an example for the generations that follow." This makes the first-generation students responsibilities sound like an honorary opportunity. As a child, bringing home a report card smothered in A's was my defining feature. I lived for the feeling of success, and at the first mention of college I knew I was expected to go and make my family proud. The very opportunities that were an incredible were also the stem of my deepest fears. I had no idea what the expectations and commitments I needed to attain in college; the secrets of passing a difficult class and finding a pathway were unknown to me. I didn't know then what it really meant to be a first-generation college student. Considering a major brought more questions than I was prepared to answer, and the possibilities were endless.

In the months leading up to the first semester, I was overwhelmed with apprehension. I struggled with the endless questions, dead ends, the fear of falling short, and not knowing the line between passion and major. My fresh first-generation knowledge left me unknowing of the height of the expectations. I came to campus searching for answers, but I hadn't realized I had already found them in the brick, wood and glass which created the campus of The University of Michigan.

I still didn't know my major at the time when my foot hit the cool morning asphalt on the University of Michigan campus for orientation in late July 2019. I was a new student on a bustling campus full of opportunities and possibilities. To say I was overwhelmed would be correct, however I had assured myself it was okay to still be undecided on my major. My heart was racing in my chest and I felt fresh new fears that would only be cured by long informational sessions about why this was a good decision. Even then the end of orientation held the terrifying event of class registrations. I calmed myself, by taking in the beauty of campus and trying to find something to connect me to this vast new place. I walked into East Quad with my bags in hand, I settled in the lounge and looked up, and I saw it.

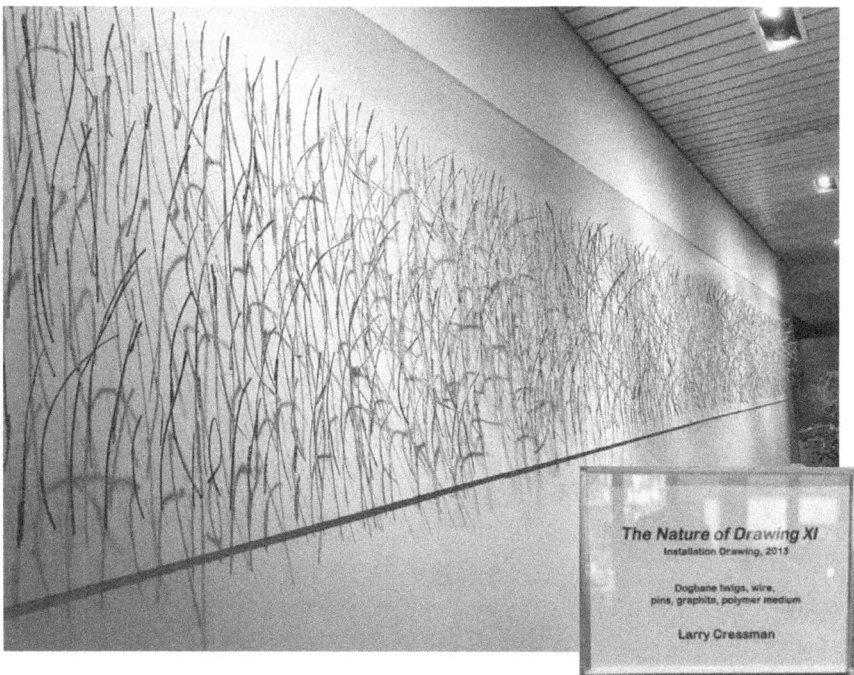

The Nature of Drawing XI
Installation Drawing, 2013

Dogbane twigs, wire, pins, graphite, polymer medium

Larry Cressman

I knew immediately it was a relation to the installation at the children's hospital. Seeing another Nature of Drawing installation would generally just be a coincidence I would brush off. However, I felt the connection again. This installation was impressive, familiar and comforting. Something about the soft bend of each twig and the way they fit into each other was a unique art of nature. My mind knew the twigs were never anticipated to be arranged like this, but the elegant puzzle they created was peaceful, clean. I felt like this was my piece of the University I knew; I saw the Nature of Drawings VII and XI as my own insider secrets. I felt as if I was one of those twigs. A twig that once was a part of a tree in a different town, a different environment. I had been living my own life on my own tree. Now I was in East Hall. Surrounded by other students from all corners of the world. I was among all the other twigs and it was art. I was not connected to the University by alumni, parents, or relatives; I was connected by twigs.

The Nature of Drawing installations helped inspire me to look for more art that made me fall in love with the campus. Throughout orientation my head was pointed up, my eyes following each line and peak of the buildings. Sunlight

View from my daily walk during orientation

bounced off the top of my forehead and reflected onto the walls of brick rising up beside me. Despite the summer temperatures threatening to choke me, I still felt chills.

Along with the chills, I still felt doubts about myself. There was pressure to impress and be successful as a first-generation college student, and I knew that in addition to my own education I was setting a precedent for my own children in the future. I was also on a mission to prove my own success and worth. The immense pressure I had placed on myself was restricting, and I almost feared allowing myself to make my own decisions for fear they would be rejected. The intimidation of failure made it impossible to reach outside of comfort to pursue new passions. Even when I didn't know what I was going to study at the University of Michigan, I felt there had to be something special for me here. I carried deep emotions with me at all times. With these I felt the relief of being accepted, the fear of failing, and

Law Quadrangle –
My favorite architecture on campus

the excitingly terrifying idea of getting my degree. The emotion I held because of the simple beauty on campus meant there was a place for me. Each building on campus surrounding me in a blanket of stone and brick felt comforting. In my decision to attend Michigan, my sentiments were in the back of my mind. I could never tell anyone that one of the most important decisions in my life, where to attend university, was made almost solely because the beauty of the buildings made me cry.

After making a decision on where, I was immediately struck with the next- what? Every friend or family member asked almost immediately what I was going to study. My doubts in myself started when people pushed questions on me. I used to say I hate talking about myself, but I think what I really hate is disappointing someone when they listen to me talk about myself. I felt like deciding on a major was an enormous decision, I wanted to feel successful; I wanted to look like I had everything figured out. I didn't want to have to justify my made-up decisions with empty lies. I don't want to be a business major, and no, supply chain management does not sound fun to me. Telling anyone what I was going to study felt indefinite, so I chose to settle for the comfort of dismissing questions with "I don't know." Although I did, I just didn't see it yet.

One suffocating hot day on campus I was walking across campus to retrieve iced coffee and find valuable air conditioning. I got a call from a number not recognized by my phone, but I figured I would answer anyways. The man on the other side of the line was an admissions representative from a Los Angeles Film school. I had investigated the possibility of a Graphic Design major while applying for colleges during my senior year and added my information to the mailing list. I hesitated to answer the man, but eventually I said my name. He inquired about my interest in the LA Film School and I declined, mentioning I was already enrolled in the University of Michigan. When he asked for my major, I defaulted as I usually do, "I'm undecided." What he said next was frustrating, something along the lines of, aren't you passionate about design? Why are you not majoring in design? You are wasting time and money if you don't know what you're majoring in! I was overwhelmed and I hung up the phone.

His questions were the types I feared, but they made me realize something. I needed to find my own place at the University. I needed to find a major, one that made me happy. I kept getting caught up in my own idea of being "undecided" that I wasn't able to focus on being decided. I tossed around some ideas, but nothing felt right.

It took a dark night and letting my eyes travel to the top of the Burton Memorial Tower when I felt chills again. The warm breeze blew against my upturned face and gently guided my hair away from my eyes, almost as if it was clearing my view of the bluish-purple light glowing inside the tower. I noticed the intense quiet of the night around me. The tower stood against a dark cloudy background, like a beacon shining in a grey watercolor sky. It's powerful stance and artful construction brought tears to my eyes.

That concluded my doubts, I wanted to be able to make something like that someday. I want the lights on a beautiful clock tower to draw attention to the center of a campus. This revelation almost made me feel foolish. From all the years designing, taking pictures, drawing, binges of Rehab Addict, Fixer Upper and Property Brothers, how could I have not seen that the architecture that surrounded me was trying to tell me something? I felt even more foolish softly crying in the darkness on the sidewalk in Ingalls Mall, but the tower had almost made the decision for me. Burton Memorial Tower that night represented beauty to any normal onlooker, but to me it represented a new and exhilarating challenge.

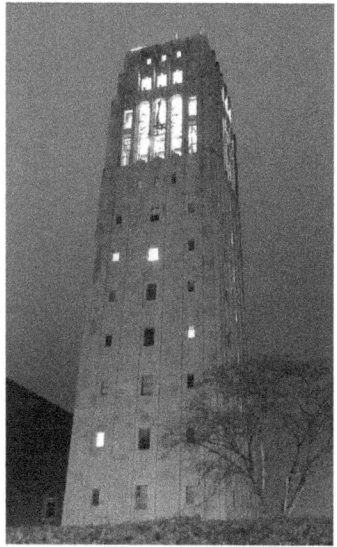

I took initiative with purpose, almost as if I was invigorated with the same wonder and anxiety I possessed on the first day of orientation. After the first few tumultuous weeks of school I had found something that gave me excitement, hope and purpose. I had almost no question that it my decision was the right one, but I still searched for validation. I have always struggled with my expectations for myself and the expectations that others hold for me. I know my parents mean well when they encourage me to be a doctor or a lawyer. I understand they want the best for me when I mention a major and they ask about the average salary, but sometimes it feels like following a path influenced by my own passions will be letting down the people in my life who have shown me the most love and support.

To face the questions that I knew were soon to come. I conducted research.

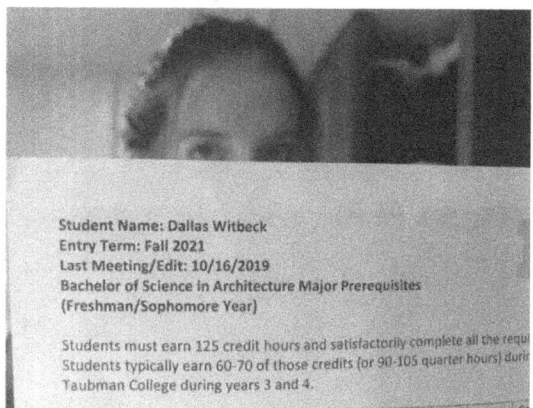

Student Name: Dallas Witbeck
Entry Term: Fall 2021
Last Meeting/Edit: 10/16/2019
Bachelor of Science in Architecture Major Prerequisites
(Freshman/Sophomore Year)

Students must earn 125 credit hours and satisfactorily complete all the requi
Students typically earn 60-70 of those credits (or 90-105 quarter hours) duri
Taubman College during years 3 and 4.

Prerequisites - on my mirror as a reminder

Within my research I found mixed reviews, but I knew that my determination would be enough to carry me through the challenges that studying architecture would bring. A strong sense of responsibility and pride originates in most first-generation students. When I made my decision, I knew the commitment was enormous. I read countless blogs and articles, the architect Shelley Little, writes, "a career in architecture requires a life-time commitment to continued education." Architecture also demands a long list of skills combined with hours of labor to succeed, as well as mentioning the not so glamorous salary (Little). I figured the only way to prove my dedication and commitment to succeed as an architect, I have to do it. I am committed to working hard to make myself and my family proud, as well as to create my own belonging in a new community of college students and more specifically architecture students.

When I met with the Architecture advisor for the Taubman College of Architecture and Urban planning, she casually asked me why I'd like to be an architect. When she asked me that question I wasn't afraid to answer. In the moment, I surprised myself with my own confidence in my answer. It was the next question I knew everyone would be asking me. I couldn't tell her about the

twigs, and I could never tell her about my emotions about the Memorial Tower. I felt the chills again. I answered carefully, I tried to not let her hear the catch in my voice that would reveal my strong emotions. I want to use my passion to make a life for myself. I want to graduate with a degree that makes people proud, and I want to make art with buildings that makes people want to cry.

I entered the Taubman College of Architecture feeling like an imposter. Surely someone would know I am just a dreamer exploring what I someday wish to be. However close I was to the beginning of my first architecture class at UofM in the next semester, I was far from being an architecture student. I knew in order to secure a spot in the program it would take the next few years to build an impressive portfolio and apply for a cross campus transfer. The next steps to validate my position as a real architecture student weighed on my mind as I walked through the building. The building itself held characteristics I found to be comforting. Sketches and renders from students covered the walls.

Interesting furniture, staircases, and even the staircase railings caught my attention. I tried to take photos discreetly, so I didn't look like a tourist. But soon I was shamelessly snapping photos of every surface of the building. Everywhere I turned was a new wall covered in art, or a new sculpture that inspired new ideas in my own

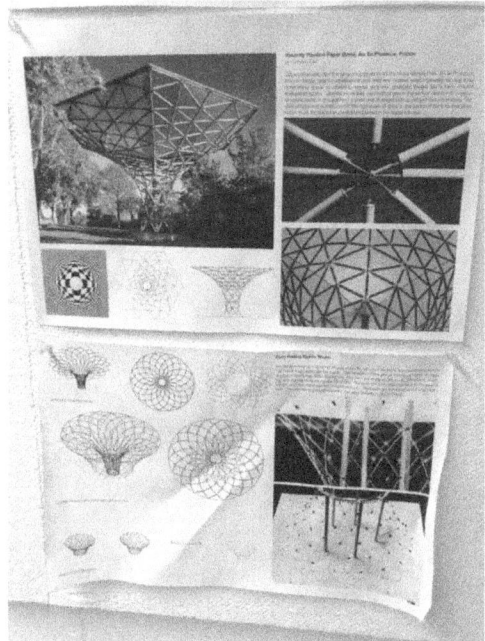

Student drawings - inspiration

mind. It seemed almost dangerous that something could make me so happy and hopeful for a career. My solo visit to Taubman made everything seem less daunting. I shared the feelings with myself, I was spared the prying questions of what-next?

and I allowed myself to think. The years of studying, creating, designing and working didn't scare me. It felt liberating. The pure, paralyzing anxiety I had as failing and disappointing, especially as a first-generation student, seemed to be repelled by a serious desire to pursue a career.

Works Cited

Little, Shelley. "10 Things Every Architecture Student Needs to Know Now." Freshome.com, 25 Nov. 2019, freshome.com/10-things-every-architecture-student-needs-to-know-now/.

"Student Life - Research." What Proportion of UM Students Are First Generation? Student Life - Research, studentlife.umich.edu/research/article/what-proportion-um-students-are-first-generation-4.

www.ingramcontent.com/pod-product-compliance
Lightning Source LLC
LaVergne TN
LVHW021402080426
835508LV00020B/2417